Conversations with Isaac Asimov

Literary Conversations Series

Peggy Whitman Prenshaw
General Editor

Photo credit: © Photofest

Conversations with
Isaac Asimov

Edited by
Carl Freedman

University Press of Mississippi
Jackson

www.upress.state.ms.us

The University Press of Mississippi is a member of the
Association of American University Presses.

First edition 2005
∞
Library of Congress Cataloging-in-Publication Data

Asimov, Isaac, 1920–
    Conversations with Isaac Asimov / edited by Carl Freedman.—1st ed.
      p. cm.— (Literary conversations series)
    Includes bibliographical references and index.
    ISBN 1-57806-737-5 (alk. paper) — ISBN 1-57806-738-3 (pbk. : alk. paper)
      1. Asimov, Isaac, 1920– —Interviews. 2. Authors, American—20th century—
Interviews. 3. Science fiction—Authorship. I. Freedman, Carl Howard.
II. Title. III. Series.

  PS3551.S5Z465   2005
  813′.54—dc22   2004061197

British Library Cataloging-in-Publication Data available

Contents

Introduction

Isaac Asimov was one of the most popular American authors of the twentieth century and quite possibly the most prolific. Furthermore, whereas most extremely prolific authors tend to concentrate their efforts almost exclusively on a single kind of book (Agatha Christie's detective novels, Louis L'Amour's Westerns), Asimov spanned many genres as well as individual titles. He wrote mystery stories and bawdy limericks, satire and autobiography. This life-long atheist wrote more than half a dozen books about the Bible, and this intellectual whose original youthful ambition was to become an academic historian wound up writing nearly twenty books of history. He published a quite successful two-volume companion to Shakespearean drama and copiously annotated editions of literary classics by Milton, Swift, and Byron. Of course, not all of Asimov's work is of equal value; a good deal of unevenness is inevitable in a lifetime output measured in the hundreds of titles. But I have never encountered an Asimov text that I found without interest. For one thing, Asimov mastered almost from the start the "simple" ability (if it were truly simple, it would be much more widely displayed than it is) to engage the reader's attention, to write prose in such a way that the reader, regardless of his or her previous attraction to the subject-matter, wants to keep turning the pages.

The great bulk of Asimov's work falls into two distinct but not unrelated genres: science fiction and popular science writing. And it is his contributions to these fields that, on the whole, account for his place in literary history.

Asimov's first fame was as a science-fiction author, and his involvement with the genre endured from childhood until old age. As a child working in his family's Brooklyn candy store, Asimov was irresistibly attracted by the rack of pulp magazines that the store offered for sale. He was especially fascinated by the science-fiction magazines that entered the literary market-place when Hugo Gernsback launched the pioneering *Amazing Stories* in 1926; and, growing up in the 1920s and 1930s, Asimov became a member of the first generation of readers who thought of themselves as science-fiction fans.

They were an unusually thoughtful and intense group, as readers of the pulps went; and they tended to think of their favorite genre as central to their lives in ways that readers of crime fiction or Westerns generally did not. Asimov was one of the many fans of his era who attempted to make the leap from reader to writer; but he made it with nearly unparalleled success. He was a published author of science-fiction stories before he was out of his teens.

Asimov's first stories were published in 1939, just two years after John W. Campbell, who became the most legendary science-fiction editor of all time, took over the editorship of *Astounding*—which, thanks to him, became the most consequential of all the science-fiction pulps. Campbell was determined to raise the quality of pulp science fiction from its hitherto abysmal literary (and scientific) standards, and to this end he recruited a cohort of authors who, under his leadership, effectively remade the genre. No one was more central to Campbell's project nor more fiercely loyal to Campbell personally than Asimov. Along with such other authors as Lester del Rey, Robert Heinlein, Henry Kuttner, C. L. Moore, Clifford D. Simak, Theodore Sturgeon, and A. E. van Vogt, Asimov, almost immediately upon his arrival on the scene, was moving in the forefront of the field. But it soon became evident that Asimov was more, even, than just one member of a talented group. By the end of the 1940s—the decade that saw magazine publication of his first robot stories and of most of the material that later made up the *Foundation* trilogy—Asimov was securely established as one of the "Big Three" of science fiction: along with Heinlein and van Vogt at first, and later, as van Vogt's productivity waned, along with Heinlein and the British author Arthur C. Clarke. In terms of general popularity, Asimov, Heinlein, and Clarke never lost their status as the Big Three.

In literary-critical terms, however, science fiction underwent further changes that must be understood in order to appreciate Asimov's place in the history of the field. As Asimov and his colleagues in the Campbell cohort remade and re-invigorated science fiction in the 1940s, so in the late 1960s and 1970s another (more loosely associated) group of writers redefined the genre again. These writers—such as Philip K. Dick, Ursula Le Guin, Samuel Delany, Thomas M. Disch, Joanna Russ, and others—were far more rooted in modern literature (and, sometimes, modern philosophy) than earlier science-fiction authors had been, and they tended to be considerably more ambitious and accomplished as stylists and as explorers of psychological and political problems. In a field that had usually been characterized by serviceable prose, straightforward narrative, and often interchangeable characters, the newcomers added a huge dose of literary sophistication. In a field that had traditionally attracted more than its share of juvenile readers (the over-whelmingly majority male), their work was unmistakably written for adults of both sexes. Compared to such groundbreaking masterpieces as Dick's *Ubik* (1969), Le Guin's *The Left Hand of Darkness* (1969) and *The Dispossessed* (1974), Russ's *The Female Man* (1975), and Delany's *Dhalgren* (1975), even the best work of the Big Three forever looks somewhat callow and primitive.

Since changes of this sort are often accompanied by considerable personal rancor and pain, it is pleasant to reflect that such was *not*, on the whole, the case with science fiction, and certainly not as far as Asimov himself was con-cerned. He maintained friendly relations with several of the younger writers (such as Delany and Harlan Ellison), and generally wished their enterprise well, even while clearly recognizing that he was not and could not be a part of it. Perhaps the most consequential single publication for the advent of the newer sort of science fiction was Ellison's strategically titled anthology *Dangerous Visions* (1967). Ellison invited Asimov to contribute a story, but Asimov declined, feeling he had nothing to offer that would be really appro-priate. Instead he contributed a foreword (or, actually, two forewords), in which he praised and tried to explain what he called the "second revolution" in science fiction while also insisting that he belonged inescapably to the "first revolution"—the Campbell revolution—himself. I do not think that anyone has ever managed to convey the contrast more vividly in two sen-tences than Asimov did: "When Campbell started his revolution, the new writers who came into the field carried with them the aura of the university, of science and engineering, of slide rule and test tube. Now the new authors who enter the field bear the mark of the poet and the artist, and somehow carry with them the aura of Greenwich Village and the Left Bank." There was never any question as to which group Asimov himself (who once dedicated a book to his slide rule) belonged to.

But the fact that Asimov frequently admitted, from the late 1960s onwards, that his science fiction was and always would be rather old-fashioned should not be mistaken for a symptom of excessive modesty: a character flaw of which Asimov was suspected by no one, least of all himself. He often added, with perfect accuracy, that, old-fashioned as his stories and novels might be, a great many people continued to enjoy them. For our part, we should not allow the fact that a second revolution in science fiction now lies between us

and Asimov—and, as some (though not I myself) would insist, a third revolution too, namely the cyberpunk movement inaugurated by William Gibson
with *Neuromancer* (1984)—to distract us from the enduring value and
immense influence of Asimov's finest work in the field. Asimov's best science
fiction includes, at a bare minimum, *I, Robot* (1950), a brilliant cycle of connected short stories that effectively redefined our conception of the robot
and whose influence can be seen in practically every robot created in science
fiction for more than half a century; the three volumes of the original
Foundation trilogy (*Foundation* [1951], *Foundation and Empire* [1952], and
Second Foundation [1953]), a vast tale of galactic scope whose vitalizing
impact is registered in such works of mass culture as the *Star Trek* and *Star
Wars* franchises, but also in such a high literary masterpiece as Delany's *Stars
in My Pocket Like Grains of Sand* (1984); *The End of Eternity* (1955), a somewhat atypical but haunting novel about time travel and the paradoxes of time
travel, which a significant minority of critics have always considered Asimov's
best fiction; *The Naked Sun* (1957), the finest of his science-fiction mysteries,
a sub-genre Asimov invented and of which he remains the undisputed master; and *The Gods Themselves* (1972), perhaps his most artfully constructed
single novel, which, though quintessentially Asimovian in many ways, also
shows, especially in its treatment of environmental and sexual themes, that
he was not completely unable or unwilling to learn from younger colleagues
like Delany and Le Guin. This is a mightily impressive record. More than a
decade after his death, Asimov's popularity remains large and intense, and he
continues to receive serious attention from serious critics as well. Though it
is impossible to predict what the future holds for science fiction (or anything
else), it seems a safe bet that in 2039 his name and work will still have sufficient currency that some will mark that year as the 100th anniversary of
Asimov's first publications in the genre.

    Yet, after the earlier years of his career, science fiction was not the field
into which Asimov directed most of his creative energy. The bulk of his work
is science writing, and his achievement here is, I think, even more impressive
than in science fiction. Science writing is a genre with a slighter and less
widely understood history than science fiction, and, in order to understand
something of the field in which Asimov made his greatest mark, it is necessary to recall some elementary but often neglected facts about the history of
science itself.

Science is so obviously and inescapably central to the world we know today that we tend to forget just how recent a development this is. The eighteenth century, for instance, was a period of considerable progress for scientific research, especially in chemistry; but relatively few contemporary observers considered this a particularly important fact about their times. Dr. Samuel Johnson, who possessed perhaps the keenest literary mind in eighteenth-century England, is an interesting example here. As it happens, Johnson had a strong personal interest in chemistry, even performing serious chemical experiments in his home. But he took it for granted that such interests could never be among the most important for the rational, educated person. He seems to have regarded his chemical experiments as what would later be called a hobby, and, if he had ever been asked why he felt natural science to be relatively unimportant in the great scheme of things, he would almost certainly have said much the same that a sanely balanced person today would say about a passion for hobbies like baseball or chess or stamp collecting: namely, that, however fascinating it might be within its own narrow limits, it had little connection to life in general and hardly anything to teach us about most of the issues that are most crucial for human beings. Science, it seemed obvious, could be intellectually interesting but was irretrievably marginal, morally, spiritually, and, perhaps above all, *practically*. A few decades before Johnson, Swift had mercilessly ridiculed scientific speculation, because it was, as he assumed, incapable of making things happen in the real world, incapable, in his famous (or infamous) example, of making two blades of grass grow where one had grown before.

Today, of course, the charge of practical uselessness is the absolute *last* charge anyone would lay against science; in the years since Swift and Johnson, the enormous impact of science upon human life has grown more and more obvious. Much of that impact, of course, has been in the form of scientifically based technology, from electrification (arguably the most consequential new technology since the invention of agriculture some ten millennia ago) and railways in the nineteenth century to the automotive, aviation, nuclear, electronic, and cybernetic technologies of the twentieth century and beyond. But science has impressed itself on everyday life in directly moral and ideological as well as technological ways. Here the outstanding nineteenth-century example is the challenge that evolutionary biology posed to the Book of Genesis, a challenge whose echoes can be heard in debates today over cloning, stem-cell research, and other bioethical matters;

and then too, there has been an enormous literature on the ethical implications posed by nuclear energy, especially in its military applications.

Unfortunately, as science has become more and more important in its effects on us all, it has also become increasingly difficult to understand without years of specialized training. As late as the nineteenth century, the concept of general education was still something more than (what it is today) a confidence trick spun by university administrators hoping to impress gullible, tuition-paying parents. It was still possible then for the ordinary educated person to possess some genuine competence in both scientific and literary subjects. But there were also, indeed, signs that this state of affairs was nearing an end. One such sign was the famous Victorian debate between Thomas Henry Huxley and Matthew Arnold about the relative claims that science and the traditional literary humanities had on the future of British education; but then again, it is also worth recalling that Huxley and Arnold themselves were men of considerable humanistic *and* scientific learning. The real Rubicon was crossed in the first decades of the twentieth century with the advent of modern physics, especially Einsteinian relativity and quantum mechanics. From this point onwards, the language of science became more and more remote from the language actually used by even the most intelligent and well-educated men and women. Increasingly, indeed, and especially in physics, language itself has been supplemented and sometimes even overshadowed in modern scientific discourse by esoteric mathematical symbolism.

So it is that, over the last century or so, the need for good, widely comprehensible science writing—science writing of genuine distinction both as science *and* as writing—has become increasingly urgent just as the task of producing such work has become increasingly difficult. Despite the difficulty, the need has in fact been abundantly met. Most observers, I think, would agree that science writing today forms one of the liveliest and most aesthetically rewarding areas of contemporary English prose; Gregory Benford, Richard Dawkins, Freeman Dyson, Richard Feynman, Martin Gardner, Stephen Jay Gould, Brian Greene, Stephen Hawking, Roald Hoffmann, Matt Ridley, Oliver Sacks, Carl Sagan, and Steven Weinberg constitute only a fraction of the currently or recently active science writers whose names might be cited in support of the proposition. Of course, no particular individual can be assigned full credit for this flourishing. But a strong argument can be made that Asimov (whom Sagan praised as the greatest *explainer* of his era— a characterization that can hardly be improved upon) deserves more credit than any other single writer, and that he remains in many ways the pivotal figure in the history of the genre.

Not, of course, that he was anything like the first science writer. In a certain sense that title probably belongs to Aristotle (for his lost exoteric writings); and the modern line that includes Asimov goes back at least as far as Huxley, and includes Huxley's most noteworthy student, H. G. Wells—who anticipated not only Asimov but also Clarke in attaining fame in both science fiction and science writing. In the U.S., Asimov's older contemporary (and fellow immigrant from Russia) George Gamow had produced more than half a dozen important books of science writing before Asimov had produced one. What sets Asimov in a class by himself is the sheer magnitude of his achievement; and this in turn is due, I think, mainly to four factors: the readability of Asimov's prose, the breadth of his knowledge, the volume of his output, and, in consequence of these three factors, his worldly success and popularity.

Asimov's virtually unfailing ability to write absorbing prose meant that he could attract readers to topics that they had never particularly supposed themselves to be interested in. Though Asimov's straightforward, unadorned writing seems to flow with the utmost ease—and although, from all the accounts of his professional habits, it *did* actually come to him quite easily—anyone who thinks it is generally easy to produce page-turning books on subjects like algebra, the neutrino, or the use of the slide rule will probably abandon the notion upon trying to emulate such achievements. At least equally impressive as the quality of his writing was Asimov's ability to produce it on a wider range of scientific issues than any other science writer, before or since. To be sure, some have criticized Asimov's knowledge of science as relatively superficial; and it is true that, unlike many (though by no means all) of the other major science writers, Asimov never became a scientist of real distinction. He worked in the academy for a few years as a Ph.D. biochemist and, by all accounts, was outstanding as a teacher and lecturer; but on the research side his talents, as he later admitted, were mediocre at best. Yet what he lacked in depth he made up in breadth, attaining a familiarity with a range of scientific subjects rare among scientists and non-scientists alike. Among physicists he may have been rather an ignoramus in physics, as in zoology among zoologists. But there were never many physicists who knew as much zoology as Asimov did, and *vice versa*.

Perhaps the most outstanding single feature of Asimov as an author is the plain bulk of his canon; and science writing is by far the largest segment of it.

Though no single volume of Asimov's science writing ever became an official bestseller, the collective impact of the millions of copies of the dozens upon dozens of compellingly written titles on an immense variety of scientific topics has been simply incommensurate to the achievement of any other writer in the field. As Sagan's tribute implies (from an author who Asimov once suggested had outstripped him as America's finest science writer), Asimov became the premier inspiration and role model for others. His success, furthermore, was not a matter only of the unprecedented personal wealth and fame that Asimov's science writing brought him. In addition, Asimov became something like Mr. Science for the American public: a generally persuasive spokesman for science and the scientific outlook on a level that, with the arguable exception of Wells, no other science writer in the English language has ever attained. Though there were always many scientists more distinguished in the laboratory than Asimov, none has ever managed to explain both the intrinsic fascination and the operational importance of science in so widely and keenly effective a way.

Asimov's genius as a great explainer (manifest, it should be noted, in the brilliant career as a public speaker that he pursued alongside his career as a writer) made him a natural subject for interviewers. The lucidity displayed in the pieces that follow should come as no surprise. Nor is it surprising that the two major subjects discussed are science and science fiction; in the latter case it is Asimov's own work in the genre that he mainly addresses, while in the former it is less the details of any particular science than the general relations between science and society. What *may* seem somewhat surprising about these conversations with Isaac Asimov is that there are so relatively few of them. Why should someone whose talents were so suited to the interview form have so generally avoided it—especially inasmuch as the demand for Asimov interviews was always considerable, from the 1960s until his death in 1992?

"I hate giving interviews," he confesses in one interview; and upon reflection the reasons why are not, I think, difficult to infer. In the first place, Asimov, as he repeatedly made clear (and his total literary productivity stands as awesome evidence of the fact), loved writing above all other things. He wrote all day, every day, to the maximum extent feasible; and, despite his famously jovial good humor, he tended to resent anything and anyone that interrupted his writing. He seems, indeed, to have felt at least a little consternation even when the point of the interruption was a convivial luncheon with old friends, or spending time with his much beloved second wife. How much more must he have resented the intrusions of total strangers seeking to interview him—who, moreover, wanted him to do something that was very *like* writing but was not actually writing itself? Here, I think, we need to consider not only the fact that Asimov was a writer but also the kind of writer he was. An unprolific author of difficult, frequently misunderstood books might welcome the opportunity to speak to the public more directly than the work itself speaks. But Asimov must have felt that the offer to be interviewed was essentially an offer to do much the same sort of thing that he could do—and daily *did* do—as well or better all by himself. Born in poverty and never one to underestimate the importance of the material rewards of his craft, Asimov must also have reflected that, unlike writing (or public speaking), being interviewed generally does not pay.

So it may, in fact, actually be a bit surprising that this volume contains as many items as it does. I cannot claim that the material below will hold many surprises for readers already well acquainted with Asimov's work, especially his science writing. As with most of Asimov's work in both fiction and nonfiction, the pleasures and rewards of reading this volume will be very similar to the pleasures and rewards of a great many of his other volumes. The number of different topics brought together here does, however, make this book not quite like any other. In particular, I do not think that, outside of his autobiographical volumes, one could easily find another book in which Asimov discusses both science and science fiction as extensively as he does here. The interviews below have of course been left unaltered from their original appearances (save that the first item, originally a conversation among several parties, the transcript of which was edited by Thomas D. Clareson, has been further edited to eliminate some material irrelevant to Asimov's participation); and this has inevitably made for a certain amount of overlap and repetition. But even the repetition may have its own point; it is always interesting to notice the particular questions that a writer tends to be asked and the consistency (or not) of his replies.

It pleases me to think of how Asimov himself might regard this book if— contrary to his own assumptions on the matter and to mine—he were somehow able to be aware of it. As I discuss elsewhere in this volume, Asimov was rather obsessed with counting the number of titles he produced. I like to think, because of the clarity and consistency of the voice with which he speaks out on such a wide variety of topics, he would have counted this title as yet one more book with even more than his usual gusto.

* * *

The more one lives, the clearer it becomes that there are no individual achievements, only collective ones; and there are doubtless many people who have contributed to this book in one way or another. For instance, I should acknowledge some excellent last-minute assistance from Carl Gardner, Professor of Mathematics at Arizona State University, who serves as the chief science adviser to all my work. But there are four persons whose contributions to this volume have been not just useful but indispensable.

The first and most important (though the least direct) contribution was made many years ago by my father (to whom this volume, to the extent that I can claim it as mine, is dedicated). When I was about twelve or thirteen years old, he suggested that I might like to read some Isaac Asimov. I did, and instantly became a devoted fan, first of Asimov's science fiction, then (and perhaps even more eagerly) of Asimov's science writing. In retrospect, the collocation of my father and Asimov does not look entirely fortuitous. My father was born about eighteen months after Asimov and, like him, came from an urban Jewish proletarian background, though in Baltimore rather than New York City. In their younger years both men were typical in many ways of the young American working-class intellectual of that era, with their characteristic heavy reliance on the public library. Both went on to live classically American stories of upward mobility. Born and raised in the working class during a time when higher education was, for the most part, still the preserve of the moneyed elite, they both managed to earn doctorates in chemistry from prestigious private universities (Johns Hopkins in my father's case, Columbia in Asimov's). From this point onwards, the parallels between them begin to fade somewhat, and certainly the differences are at least as striking as any similarities. My father became a better scientist than Asimov, and also an infinitely better father; and he has always been a much more normal sort of person than Asimov, from all the biographical and autobiographical evidence, seems ever to have been. Asimov, of course, became a far more important writer. Still, they remain linked in my mind by a certain shared quality of noble rationality—an orientation that has doubtless left its mark on my own outlook and work, not least in the current volume.

Nearly any book, I imagine, owes a considerable debt to its editor, but I feel sure that Seetha Srinivasan, the director of the University Press of Mississippi, deserves a larger than typical share of the credit for this one. I once commented to her that one lack in the justly well-known Literary Conversations series published by her press was the absence of any science-fiction writers.

I did not intend this to be anything more than a casual, inconsequential remark, but Seetha took the lead in developing the idea that eventually became this book. The project would never have come to fruition, or anything close to it, without her support and encouragement.

Finally, it is difficult to find the words that adequately express my debt to my two research assistants at Louisiana State University, Sharon Joyce and Ilana Xinos. Between them, they performed the bulk of the sterner labor that made this volume possible—locating the interviews, securing the permissions to reprint, and the like—but what they both proved is that such labor is not, in fact, as purely mechanical as one might suppose. It requires intelligence and imagination in addition to diligence and industry, and both Sharon and Ilana supplied all these qualities in abundance.

CF

Chronology

1920	Born on January 2 in Petrovichi, Russia, to Judah and Anna Rachel (Berman) Asimov.
1923	Arrives in the United States with his parents on February 23.
1928	Becomes an American citizen in September.
1931	Begins to write a (never finished and eventually lost) novel entitled "The Greenville Chums in College"; at this point first begins to think of himself as a writer.
1932–1935	Attends Brooklyn's elite Boys High School; graduates at age fifteen.
1935–1936	Attends Seth Low Junior College (an undergraduate college of Columbia University).
1936–1939	Attends Columbia College.
1939	Graduates from Columbia with a B.S. in chemistry; begins publishing stories in science-fiction magazines; begins postgraduate work at Columbia University.
1942	Marries Gertrude Blugerman on July 26.
1942–1945	Works at the Naval Air Experimental Station in Philadelphia.
1945	Receives draft notice on September 7.
1945–1946	Serves in the U.S. Army.
1946	Receives "research discharge" from the Army to continue his postgraduate studies on July 26.
1948	Receives Ph.D. in chemistry from Columbia University.
1948–1949	Postdoctoral student at Columbia.
1950	Publishes his first book, the science-fiction novel *Pebble in the Sky*.
1950–1951	Instructor in biochemistry, Boston University School of Medicine.
1951–1958	Assistant professor of biochemistry, Boston University School of Medicine.
1951	Son David born on August 20.

1954	Publishes his first book of science writing, *The Chemicals of Life.*
1955	Daughter Robyn born on February 19.
1956	Meets Janet Opal Jeppson.
1970	Legally separates from Gertrude Asimov; moves from Boston back to New York City on July 3.
1973	Divorces Gertrude Asimov; marries Janet Opal Jeppson on November 30.
1987	Wins Grandmaster Award from the Science Fiction Writers of America.
1992	Dies from heart and kidney failure on April 6.

Books by Isaac Asimov

With most writers, compiling a list of books produced is a fairly straightforward matter; with Isaac Asimov, it is anything but. Asimov was probably the most prolific writer of his era and conceivably the most prolific writer of all time. In addition, he was much occupied with the *idea* of being prolific; Asimov seems to have counted his books with something of the same fierce obsessiveness with which a serious collector counts the number of coins or baseball cards stashed away, or with which a Don Juan counts the number of women seduced. The parallels are instructive: For one thing, though these types are notoriously prone to exaggeration, collectors, on the whole, really do have an astonishing number of collectibles in their closets, and Don Juans are not noted for the practice of celibacy. In the comments that follow, I am much indebted to the bibliographic spade work in David Bratman, "How Many Books Wrote Isaac Asimov?," the *New York Review of Science Fiction*, March 1996, pp. 21–23—though I have not followed Bratman's reasoning at every point.

Asimov's own final reckoning claims 470 books produced, and there are at least eleven posthumously published books (including this one) that he almost certainly would have claimed, bringing the grand total to about 481. This is a stupendous figure. It amounts to between six and seven books annually for every year of his life; or, if one begins counting not from his birth in 1920 but from the publication of his first book in 1950, then the average is nearly a book *every month* thereafter, until his death in 1992. It is hard to think of any other writer, of any sort and in any time or place, who rivals this record of productivity.

But the count of 481 books is in some ways misleading. Asimov strained to include as many titles on his list as possible, and he was abetted by publishers eager, for the sake of sales and even on the smallest pretext, to put his name on the covers of as many of their books as they could. The 481 include—for instance—anthologies for which most of the real editorial work was performed by co-editors; nominally co-authored books to which Asimov's contribution was, often by his own admission, minimal; repackagings of material (mainly stories and essays) that had already appeared in book form but not in precisely the same combinations and permutations; new editions of old books, with slightly altered titles; single stories or essays republished as freestanding pamphlets and chapbooks; and several other categories that might be regarded as at least somewhat problematic. The truly impressive point, though, is that, even after all such allowances have been made—even if we adopt a procedure diametrically opposed to Asimov's own, and, rather than include every book that might arguably be counted, we instead ruthlessly exclude every title save those that clearly and inarguably *must* be counted—the grand tally is still in excess of two hundred books: a figure that, one might suppose, ought to satisfy any desire to be a prolific author. It remains an interesting psychological puzzle as to why Asimov, having written so much, should have tried to give the impression of having written even more than he had. Was he unaware that exaggeration tends, at least in the long run, to undermine rather than to strengthen one's claims? Was he indeed in the grip of the sort of repetition compulsion that made no book list seem long enough (just as the collector can never have a sufficiently large collection, nor the Don Juan enough conquests)? We will never know.

In any case, the book list that follows is selective; it includes only part of the total even by the most conservative calculation of the latter. But I suspect that few readers of this volume, hungry to read more Asimov, will complain that this list is too meager. Those that *do* seek even more Asimov titles may easily consult the bibliography at the end of Asimov's posthumously published *I. Asimov: A Memoir* (New York: Doubleday, 1994).

Fiction

I, Robot. New York: Gnome Press, 1950.
Pebble In The Sky. Garden City: Doubleday, 1950.
The Stars, Like Dust. Garden City: Doubleday, 1951.
Foundation. New York: Gnome Press, 1951.
Foundation and Empire. New York: Gnome Press, 1952.
The Currents of Space. Garden City: Doubleday, 1952.
Second Foundation. New York: Gnome Press, 1953.
The Caves of Steel. Garden City: Doubleday, 1954.
The End of Eternity. Garden City: Doubleday, 1955.
The Martian Way and Other Stories. Garden City: Doubleday, 1955.
Earth Is Room Enough. Garden City: Doubleday, 1957.
The Naked Sun. Garden City: Doubleday, 1957.
Nine Tomorrows. Garden City: Doubleday, 1959.
The Rest of the Robots. Garden City: Doubleday, 1964.
Fantastic Voyage. Boston: Houghton Mifflin, 1966.
Through a Glass, Clearly. London: New English Library, 1967.
Asimov's Mysteries. Garden City: Doubleday, 1968.
Nightfall and Other Stories. Garden City: Doubleday, 1969.
Opus 100. Boston: Houghton Mifflin, 1969.
The Best New Thing. New York: World Pub. Co., 1971.
The Sensuous Dirty Old Man. New York: Walker, 1971.

The Gods Themselves. Garden City: Doubleday, 1972.

Tales of the Black Widowers. Garden City: Doubleday, 1974.

Buy Jupiter, and Other Stories. Garden City: Doubleday, 1975.

More Tales of the Black Widowers. Garden City: Doubleday/Crime Club, 1976.

Murder at The ABA. Garden City: Doubleday, 1976.

The Bicentennial Man and Other Stories. Garden City: Doubleday, 1976.

Asimov's Sherlockian Limericks. New York: Mysterious Press, 1978.

Opus 200. Boston: Houghton Mifflin, 1979.

Casebook of the Black Widowers. Garden City: Doubleday, 1980.

Foundation's Edge. Garden City: Doubleday, 1982.

The Complete Robot. Garden City: Doubleday, 1982.

The Robots of Dawn. Garden City: Doubleday, 1983.

The Union Club Mysteries. Garden City: Doubleday, 1983.

The Winds of Change and Other Stories. Garden City: Doubleday, 1983.

Banquets of the Black Widowers. Garden City: Doubleday, 1984.

Opus 300. Boston: Houghton Mifflin, 1984.

Robots and Empire. Garden City: Doubleday, 1985.

The Edge of Tomorrow. New York: T. Doherty Associates, 1985.

Foundation and Earth. Garden City: Doubleday, 1986.

Robot Dreams. New York: Berkley Books, 1986.

The Alternate Asimovs. Garden City: Doubleday, 1986.

The Best Mysteries of Isaac Asimov. Garden City: Doubleday, 1986.

Fantastic Voyage II: Destination Brain. New York: Doubleday, 1987.

Other Worlds of Isaac Asimov. New York: Avenel Books, 1987.

Azazel. New York: Doubleday, 1988.

Prelude to Foundation. New York: Doubleday, 1988.

Nemesis. New York: Doubleday, 1989.

Puzzles of the Black Widowers. New York: Doubleday, 1990.

Robot Visions. New York: Penguin Books, 1990.

Asimov Laughs Again. New York: HarperCollins, 1992.

Forward the Foundation. New York: Doubleday, 1993.

Gold. New York: HarperPrism, 1995.

Magic. New York: HarperPrism, 1996.

Nonfiction

The Chemicals of Life. New York: Abelard-Schuman, 1954.

Inside The Atom. London: Abelard-Schuman, 1956.

Building Blocks of the Universe. New York: Abelard-Schuman, 1957.

Only a Trillion. London: Abelard-Schuman, 1957.

The World of Carbon. London: Abelard-Schuman, 1958.

The World of Nitrogen. London: Abelard-Schuman, 1958.

The Clock We Live On. London: Abelard-Schuman, 1959.

The Living River. London: Abelard-Schuman, 1959.

Words of Science, and the History Behind Them. Boston: Houghton Mifflin, 1959.

Breakthroughs in Science. Boston: Houghton Mifflin, 1960.

The Intelligent Man's Guide to Science. New York: Basic Books, 1960.

The Kingdom of the Sun. London: Abelard-Schuman, 1960.

Realm of Measure. Boston: Houghton Mifflin, 1960.

Satellites in Outer Space. New York: Random House, 1960.

The Double Planet. London: Abelard-Schuman, 1960.

The Wellsprings of Life. London: Abelard-Schuman, 1960.

Realm of Algebra. Boston: Houghton Mifflin, 1961.

Words from the Myths. Boston: Houghton Mifflin, 1961.

Fact and Fancy. Garden City: Doubleday, 1962.

Life and Energy. Garden City: Doubleday, 1962.

The Search For The Elements. New York: Basic Books, 1962.

Words in Genesis. Boston: Houghton Mifflin, 1962.

Words on the Map. Boston: Houghton Mifflin, 1962.

The Genetic Code. New York: Orion Press, 1963.

The Human Body. Boston: Houghton Mifflin, 1963.

View from a Height. Garden City: Doubleday, 1963.

Words from the Exodus. Boston: Houghton Mifflin, 1963.

Adding a Dimension. Garden City: Doubleday, 1964.

Asimov's Biographical Encyclopedia of Science and Technology, 1st Ed. Garden City: Doubleday, 1964.

Quick and Easy Math. Boston: Houghton Mifflin, 1964.

The Human Brain. Boston: Houghton Mifflin, 1964.

An Easy Introduction to the Slide Rule. Boston: Houghton Mifflin, 1965.

A Short History of Chemistry. Garden City: Anchor Books, 1965.

Of Time and Space and Other Things. Garden City: Doubleday, 1965.

The New Intelligent Man's Guide to Science. New York: Basic Books, 1965.

From Earth to Heaven. Garden City: Doubleday, 1966.

Inside The Atom, 3rd revised edition. London: Abelard-Schuman, 1966.

The Neutrino: Ghost Particle of the Atom. Garden City: Doubleday, 1966.

The Noble Gases. New York: Basic Books, 1966.

Environments Out There. London: Scholastic/Abelard-Schuman, 1967.

Is Anyone There? Garden City: Doubleday, 1967.

Asimov's Guide to the Bible, Volume I. Garden City: Doubleday, 1968.

Photosynthesis. New York: Basic Books, 1968.

Science, Numbers, and I. Garden City: Doubleday, 1968.

Asimov's Guide to the Bible, Volume II. Garden City: Doubleday, 1969.

Twentieth Century Discovery. Garden City: Doubleday, 1969.

Great Ideas of Science. Boston: Houghton Mifflin, 1969.

Asimov's Guide to Shakespeare, Volume I. Garden City: Doubleday, 1970.

Asimov's Guide to Shakespeare, Volume II. Garden City: Doubleday, 1970.

The Solar System and Back. Garden City: Doubleday, 1970.

Asimov's Biographical Encyclopedia of Science and Technology, New Rev. Ed. Garden City: Doubleday, 1972.

The Stars in Their Courses. Garden City: Doubleday, 1971.

Asimov's Annotated "Don Juan". Garden City: Doubleday, 1972.

Asimov's Guide to Science. New York: Basic Books, 1972.

More Words of Science. Boston: Houghton Mifflin, 1972.

The Left Hand of the Electron. Garden City: Doubleday, 1972.

The Story of Ruth. Garden City: Doubleday, 1972.

Please Explain. Boston: Houghton Mifflin, 1973.

The Tragedy of the Moon. Garden City: Doubleday, 1973.

Today and Tomorrow and—. Garden City: Doubleday, 1973.

Asimov on Astronomy. Garden City: Doubleday, 1974.

Asimov on Chemistry. Garden City: Doubleday, 1974.

Asimov's Annotated "Paradise Lost". New York: Doubleday, 1974.

Our World in Space. Greenwich: New York Graphic Society, 1974.

Eyes on the Universe. Boston: Houghton Mifflin, 1975.

Of Matters Great and Small. Garden City: Doubleday, 1975.

Science Past, Science Future. Garden City: Doubleday, 1975.

Asimov on Physics. Garden City: Doubleday, 1976.

The Planet That Wasn't. Garden City: Doubleday, 1976.

Asimov on Numbers. Garden City: Doubleday, 1977.

Familiar Poems Annotated. Garden City: Doubleday, 1977.

The Beginning and the End. Garden City: Doubleday, 1977.

Animals of the Bible. Garden City: Doubleday, 1978.

Life and Time. Garden City: Doubleday, 1978.

Quasar, Quasar, Burning Bright. Garden City: Doubleday, 1978.

A Choice of Catastrophes. New York: Simon & Schuster, 1979.

Extraterrestrial Civilizations. New York: Crown Publishers, 1979.

In Memory Yet Green. New York: Doubleday, 1979.

Isaac Asimov's Book of Facts. New York: Grosset & Dunlap, 1979.

The Road to Infinity. Garden City: Doubleday, 1979.

The Annotated "Gulliver's Travels". New York: Clarkson N. Potter, 1980.

In Joy Still Felt. Garden City: Doubleday, 1980.

Asimov on Science Fiction. Garden City: Doubleday, 1981.

Change! Boston: Houghton Mifflin, 1981.

In the Beginning. New York: Crown Publishers, 1981.

The Sun Shines Bright. Garden City: Doubleday, 1981.

Exploring the Earth and the Cosmos. New York: Crown, 1982.

Asimov's Biographical Encyclopedia of Science and Technology, 2nd Rev. Ed. Garden City: Doubleday, 1982.

Counting the Eons. Garden City: Doubleday, 1983.

The Measure of the Universe. New York: Harper & Row, 1983.

The Roving Mind. Buffalo: Prometheus Books, 1983.

Asimov's New Guide to Science. New York: Basic Books, 1984.

X Stands for Unknown. Garden City: Doubleday, 1984.

The Exploding Suns. New York: Dutton, 1985.

The Subatomic Monster. Garden City: Doubleday, 1985.

Futuredays. New York: Henry Holt, 1986.

The Dangers of Intelligence and Other Science Essays. Boston: Houghton Mifflin, 1986.

Far as Human Eye Could See. Garden City: Doubleday, 1987.

Past, Present, and Future. Buffalo: Prometheus Books, 1987.

Asimov's Annotated Gilbert and Sullivan. New York: Doubleday, 1988.

The Relativity of Wrong. New York: Doubleday, 1988.

Asimov On Science. New York: Doubleday, 1989.

Asimov's Chronology of Science and Discovery. New York: Harper & Row, 1989.

Asimov's Galaxy. New York: Doubleday, 1989.

Frontiers. New York: Dutton, 1989.

The Tyrannosaurus Prescription. Buffalo: Prometheus Books, 1989.

Out of the Everywhere. New York: Doubleday, 1990.

The Secret of the Universe. New York: Doubleday, 1990.

Atom. New York: Dutton, 1991.

Isaac Asimov's Guide to Earth and Space. New York: Random House, 1991.

I. Asimov. New York: Doubleday, *1994.*

Yours, Isaac Asimov. New York: Doubleday, 1995.

Conversations with Isaac Asimov

Science Fiction: The New Mythology

Thomas D. Clareson / 1968

From *Extrapolation*, May 1969: 69–115. Copyright © 1969. Reprinted by permission of Mrs. Alice S. Clareson.

[Ed. Note: The M.L.A. forum on sf took place at the Americana Hotel, 29 December 1968, the third and final afternoon of the Association's annual meeting. Professor Franklin is, of course, author of *Future Perfect*; Professor Suvin, originally form Yugoslavia, is author of a forthcoming study of Eastern European sf. At this point in their distinguished careers, Isaac Asimov is science editor of *The Magazine of Fantasy and Science Fiction*, while Fred Pohl edits *Galaxy Magazine*. Miss Judith Merril was scheduled to have been a panelist but was unavoidably detained. Nor should it be forgotten that Professor Scott Osborn of Mississippi State had the original task of organizing the forum.

The following article derives from a transcript of the tape of the full two and half hour forum. In editing it, I have used a blue pencil as lightly as possible, particularly in the discussion coming after the formal presentation of papers, in order to preserve as much of the flavor of immediate participation as possible. At all times I have sought to eliminate only those hesitations and repetitions which naturally occur during unrehearsed presentation; however, where those repetitions, for example, have seemed necessary to capture some nuance of meaning or opinion, I have retained them. Because I was working from a tape, I must assume all responsibilities for such matters as punctuation and sentence structure and hope the speakers will forgive me.

There are only two major deviations from the tape. Professor Suvin sent me a copy of his paper, suggesting that I use it because, as both he and Franklin pointed out, his task of introducing a comparatively unfamiliar field—Soviet sf—required more time than he had available as a panelist, though he was given additional time. However, in those instances when he added to, or changed significantly, some passage of the paper at the forum,

I have included that material, indicating its presence with []s. Secondly, I have eliminated Franklin's brief introductions of the speakers. Except for these two factors, however, I have tried to reproduce an exact transcription.

To emphasize the historical importance of the forum to the critical recognition of science fiction is to belabor the obvious. Certainly the divergent approaches to the genre expressed during the course of the forum indicate both how thoroughly sf is an integral part of modern thought and literature and not only the wide range for possible future study, but, more important, the wide range possible for future writing of this newest mythology.]

Bruce Franklin (after preliminary announcements): Now I think that this forum is not unconnected with what's going on at the Americana Hotel right now at the business meeting and what has been occurring throughout this convention. When we first started the science fiction seminar, that itself was an act which was considered by most people in the profession who knew about it very eccentric, radical, perhaps even lunatic. That I think is a fair statement. And as that seminar has developed and we have moved toward something like this forum, it has been necessary to present many arguments about the legitimacy of this area in our field. The issues, I think, some of them, have very closely to do with the issues being debated here: that is, about the relevancy of literature to life, and the whole question of what kind of literature is appropriate to be taught in colleges and universities. The thing, of course, which made science fiction not respectable was that it was a popular art form. It has been from the beginning—certainly of modern science fiction—a literature of the people, in many ways different from some of the other literature that we teach without raising eyebrows in the curricula of colleges and universities.[1]

Isaac Asimov: Dr. Franklin and Mr. Pohl, everybody, everybody. As is usual I come unprepared, which doesn't matter, because I am always unprepared. No

1. I feel that I must modify the implications of Franklin's opening remarks, at least so far as the governing body of the M.L.A. itself is concerned. Never has that body refused one of our petitions for a conference-seminar. When we petitioned to become a permanent group, that was not acted upon because the M.L.A. was then shifting its emphasis from groups to continuing and special seminars. Except for *E.L.T.*, we are, as a matter of fact, the oldest continuing seminar of the M.L.A. At the first conference in 1958, which I had the privilege of chairing, the panelists included Professors Charles C. Walcutt (Queens) and J. O. Bailey (North Carolina). Professor Bailey was chairman of the second conference. However, Franklin's remarks are fully accurate in describing the reactions of many of our colleagues in individual departments. Not, however, the M.L.A. as governing body.

one can tell the difference. Right? My topic, "Science Fiction and Science," can lead me in any of at least three different directions, and if I exercise sufficient ingenuity, many more, I think. But I will list the three different directions that occur to me, eliminate the two instantly, and then talk on the third.

Science fiction can serve science as a recruiting agency: in other words, science fiction can serve to interest youngsters in science, and a certain percentage of them will someday become professional scientists, and in an age which depends upon science for its salvation, and also to a certain extent, for its destruction, why this is desirable, or undesirable, according to whether salvation or destruction wins out. I know this is a proper function of science fiction because it was science fiction that recruited me to science—whether for salvation or destruction, I will leave to my friends and enemies to decide.

More important still from my viewpoint, science fiction serves as a source for science writers. I have maintained in the past that science writing is extremely important these days in order to introduce to laymen the significant advances being made by science at their expense, as taxpayers, and also to explain to one group of scientists what is being done by every other group of scientists, because, alas, in science today everybody is a layman—everybody without exception. Even those people who consider themselves and are considered professional scientists usually know at a professional level only their own small segment of the scientific panorama, and everywhere else they are only slightly better off than the overall layman. Now where are we going to find science writers? A science writer has to pass two almost insuperable barriers. He has to be reasonably competent in science—which is not easy to obtain. He also has to be reasonably competent as a writer—which is even more difficult to obtain. Therefore, to obtain people who are both reasonably competent in science and as writers is extremely difficult, and the one place where I think we can get them without difficulty is in the field of science fiction, which has the same requirements. It is no accident that a great many good science writers of today have served a certain apprenticeship in science fiction. I won't list them, except to say I am one of them.

But that leaves the third aspect of science fiction and science. Science fiction serves as a vision of the future. Ordinary scientists—I say ordinary scientists not meaning to run them down, but after all, a scientist who is only a scientist is only a scientist is only a scientist. He is not like a science-fiction writer, a man dedicated to visioning, if I may use the word. A scientist is too often lost in his own specialty and does well if he can see a little bit ahead of his specialty. A science-fiction writer, a good one, not being bound to any specialty, can look at the distant horizon with a panoramic view, of which the average scientist is deprived, sometimes by his own free will, since there is a certain danger in seeing too far in the future and too panoramically. One can easily gain the reputation of being an eccentric or to use a more professional word, "a nut." Now it is all right for me to be a nut; I have been one for many, many years now, and I am used to it. But many scientists are afraid of the phrase or word. Now in this aspect of sf, this service which it performs for science, the vision of the future, we are frequently assumed these days to have run out of ideas or at least to be overtaken by science. People are usually pretty pleased by that; at least when they approach me, they seem pleased. Nothing seems to please them more than to see me without anything to write about anymore because science "has caught up with sf." Of course people who think science has caught up with sf have never read very much sf, you understand.

I like to think of the sf writer in metaphoric terms as being bound by strong chains to the front of a locomotive which is speeding across the countryside. No matter how fast the locomotive goes, the person bound to its front sees ahead. The locomotive, no matter how fast it goes, can only catch up to what the person in front has seen in the past. It can never catch up to what he sees in the future. Admittedly, if the locomotive moves particularly quickly, it becomes a little more difficult to see clearly, but it can be done, given sufficient ingenuity. And if there is one thing that good sf writers have, it's sufficient ingenuity.

For instance, I will give you an example of a vision. Right now we are living in great days. The *Apollo 8* expedition has proven a complete success. It has fulfilled the fondest dreams of many sf readers. As a matter of fact, back in 1939 I wrote a story which I happen to remember appeared in the July 1939 issue of *Astounding.* In it I described the flight around the moon and back. It wasn't anything like the flight that just took place. The ship was built by my one-man inventor in his backyard out of beaten-up tin cans. There was no government participation. There were no officers involved. No huge NASA. No Russians. There was just my hero and his tin cans. He built his spaceship, flew it around the moon and back. There was no problem about re-entry. I'd never heard the word. He made it safely. The thing that bothers me is that it took place according to my description in 1973, and I thought I was being amazingly optimistic. I thought I was being very science-fictionish and daring. Had anyone told me at the time that it would be done by 1968 after a tremendous preparation, of which I had no concept, I would not have believed it. That's all. And yet, here it is.

But what does the future hold for us? You can read in the newspapers all the plans we have for the future. Pretty soon we are actually going to land men on the moon. Pretty soon we are going to investigate the moon, perhaps build observatories on the moon to investigate the moon, perhaps build observatories on the moon to investigate the rest of the universe. We are going to send flights past Mars and Venus to make better photographs, better experiments, than we have before. We perhaps will actually land ships on Mars and Venus. Maybe even send men towards Mars and Venus. All, all this is in one way nothing. It is still merely an extension of man's stay on Earth.

If we want a real breakthrough—the real, real breakthrough, I'll tell you what it is. It is the establishment of a colony on the moon that is not only permanent, but that is independent of the Earth. I don't mean politically independent. I mean ecologically independent. I want to see a group of people, preferably a fairly large group, living underground. It would have to be underground, I think, on the moon. They have drawn their initial investment from Earth, but now they can obtain everything they need to keep up the investment from the Moon's crust itself. They can get energy from the sun or from hydrogen fusion plants. They can get all the material they need—all the various elements—from the moon's crust, including water, from which they can obtain air. And, of course, they can establish a thoroughly cyclic ecology.

Why do I consider this the breakthrough? For three reasons: first, it would represent the first time in man's history that a segment of mankind would become independent of the Earth. It would represent the fact that man's bet is not solely dependent upon a single planet. There is a perceptible chance right now that we may ruin Earth as an abode for human life, or at least for respectable human life. There are members of congress who talk about the possibility that life will be reduced to a single Adam and Eve, and they seem to find pleasure out of the thought that perhaps this Adam and Eve may exist on the North American continent rather than in the Old World. I would consider this criminal if it were not the colossal ignorance of congressmen speaking. If we are going to wipe out life on Earth, what I want to see is an independent moon colony still capable of carrying out the human dream.

Secondly, once we can establish an ecologically independent colony on the moon, this would be the forerunner for further colonies on other planets, or bodies, like Mars—like some of the asteroids. We can then begin to have man on a plurality of worlds, of many worlds, developing cultures in many ways. And even this is only a means to an end. As long as we explore the solar system only, we still have very little. There is no place in the solar system outside Earth where men can live without expensive engineering. But out beyond this solar system are stars by the hundreds of billions, circled by planets in the hundreds of billions, of which many billions may closely resemble the Earth in chemistry and in physical properties. There may be many places where man can colonize planets very much like the Earth.

The problem is how to reach these stars out there. Now I believe that there is no way in which mankind will ever be able to go faster than the speed of light; however, that is in an objective way. We can perhaps cut down the time subjectively by, for instance, freezing the people on board a large ship heading out to the stars, so that passage of time is insignificant to them. Or else, if we obtain speeds very close to that of light, the phenomenon of time dilatation may make the experience of time passage much less, so that it would seem that stars would be reached in a matter of weeks, while on Earth years or centuries might pass. However the stars are reached, with whatever shrinkage in subjective time, time on Earth will pass in the years and centuries. It will be impossible for an astronaut heading for the distant stars to make a round trip and find the planet he has left behind. This raises certain psychological difficulties. A long trip in an enclosed spaceship, to say goodbye forever to the Earth we knew—not only is it going to make it difficult to recruit astronauts; more important, it is going to make it difficult to keep people on Earth interested in the project. To spend a lot of money to send up a spaceship which you will never see again, even if it is successful, is asking a lot of human beings.

Therefore, I don't think that Earthmen will ever successfully colonize the stars, but I think moonmen may. It will be completely different for people living in an ecologically independent colony on the moon, or on some other planet similar, because there, you see, they are not leaving the Earth behind. They are leaving a spaceship behind. People living in caverns under the moon's surface are, in essence, living in spaceships—a large spaceship which is mostly wall, and something which isn't going anywhere except circling the Earth and Earth and Earth, and then circling the sun with the Earth and so on. All you have to do is get into a somewhat smaller spaceship with somewhat thinner walls and head it outward, away from the solar system; but in a sense you are still home. You've taken it with you. Psychologically it would be much easier for a group of moon colonists to head out for the distant stars than for Earthmen, and I think for that reason the real breakthrough that is coming is the establishment of an ecologically independent moon colony. Only in that way do we stand a good chance of eventually colonizing planets of distant stars.

Though none of us in the flesh may see it, we may yet know in the spirit that, perhaps, if other intelligences have not beaten us to the punch too far and too long ago—that perhaps man may yet spread through the entire galaxy and even beyond. I have said this before. As far as I know, nobody else has, which of course means nothing. I try not to read what other people say. I have said this first in a story I published in '52; I have said it in '65 at a scientific gathering in a talk which was later printed. I say it again now; I shall continue saying it. Because I am an sf writer, people pay little attention, and I don't much care about that. People do see it occasionally. It does sink in. Other people will, like my friend, Fred Pohl, eventually quote it, forgetting I said it first. And that's all right, too. I will fulfill my function as an sf writer, as will Fred and all the other sf writers in the audience and elsewhere. In presenting their ideas—spreading it as far as they can—they will someday find fruit. And even if nobody ever says this originated because some sf writer once thought it up, even if no one ever says that, we in our hearts know it and that's enough for us.

Frederik Pohl: I think I should explain a rather obscure reference that Isaac Asimov made. In an editorial in one of my magazines a month or two ago, I quoted a remark by someone whom I identified as an unknown great man: Isaac instantly wrote me and said he had written the remark and gave me the original statement so that I could compare it. When I said that the original statement didn't look much like what he had quoted, and I wondered how he had recognized it, he said, "You said a great man."

I regret Judith Merril's absence very much for a number of reasons, one of which being that she would probably have been the only voice on this platform to have espoused the cause of that phenomenon in sf called "the new wave," which I regret because I think that it deserves a voice, and also because I enjoy rebutting any remarks that are made in this connection. Perhaps someone in the audience in the discussion period may take it up. Perhaps it has some advantage that she hasn't shown because it must be quite a confusing experience to listen to four people like Isaac and Darko, and Judith, if she had been here, and myself describe sf to you: something like the parable of the four blind men and the elephant. Darko said it's a wall, and Isaac said it's a rope; Judy might have said it was a tree, and I would have to say that I don't know what in the hell it is. But it is pretty big, and we should treat it with respect, because there are many forms of sf, none really more valid than the other.

Bruce Franklin: From the presentations we've had, I think that what I said initially has been somewhat demonstrated, but further, what has been demonstrated is that what is peculiar, perhaps almost peculiar, to science fiction is the extreme sense of relevancy of the concerns both of the authors of science fiction and of the critics of science fiction. That is, we find ourselves when we talk about science fiction getting into the problem: how in the world do we relate this subject matter to the immediate problems—the physical environment and the social environments and so forth built into the material. For that purpose I would like to see if we can start out by having any kind of meeting for these widely disparate points of view, or these confrontations, in these widely different points of view.

Fred Pohl: I don't think our points of view are really disparate at all. I think we are all talking about different aspects of the same thing. What characterizes sf to me is its enormously protean quality.

Isaac Asimov: That's absolutely so, considering the permissiveness of the stage and literature these days. I once wrote a story in which I managed to denounce mother love as obscene—which I think is a lot more difficult than just presenting naked bodies.

Darko Suvin: I would agree that we do not differ basically. I think this is, as Bruce Franklin said, something which is really built into this genre. If you want to have a good science-fiction story, novel, or whatever, I think that it is obviously a work of literature. All right, and the prevailing literary theory in the nineteenth century and what we still have with us in its echoes and in what you so politely called academe, Fred, is that literature is like an Indian reservation. All literature inside and no literature outside, you know. Everything outside is inert material which must be transmuted to a higher level of—I don't know—sentiment, emotion, what not, and then it becomes literature, losing magically in the process somehow—I never understood why or how—its real character, its connections with reality. Now science fiction insofar as it has produced valid works of literary art, and I think it obviously has produced them in fairly great quantity and good quality, denies this basic, let us say, academic stance—still basic, I think, in academe.

Isaac Asimov: I would like to call the audience's attention to one of the remarks Bob Silverberg made in the privacy of the non-microphone. He said he was without academic affiliation, and therefore, of course, we have to pay no attention to him whatsoever. It means also since I have academic affiliation that I was obviously speaking over his head. Now in my little anecdote about my backyard, tin-can spaceship, I, of course, was wrong in every possible prediction except one: I said it would happen, and that came true. Now, granted that science fiction is literature and that every point Bob Silverberg made is so well taken that I took it for granted. It still remains true that anyone who writes science fiction cannot help but predict—not that something will happen, but that something can happen, that something might happen, that it is at least fun to suppose that this sort of thing might some day happen. And if you take all of science fiction and "smush" it together and stir well, and set it down in the hot sun and wait for something to rise to the top, that top is likely to be pretty accurate prediction. This is what I'm talking about. Granted Robert thinks that this thing that rises to the top is a kind of scum, but nevertheless it can be useful.

Sophia Morgan: We've spoken about myths—people have—and about utopian societies—about the utilitarian or aesthetic aspects of things in sf. But one thing people haven't touched at all is things only sf can do. Myth is a word that exists which sf explodes, and usually the way this is done is to show that there is some kind of category trespassing. There is one story that I remember and like very much by Isaac Asimov, where he sets up a wonderful machine. The story is really hilarious, and you are completely taken in. I read the story about five times—at different times—going back to see how on earth you put words together to make the reader be so completely taken in. He sets up this machine which triggers off seeds of reaction with some new substance which has been discovered which dissolves in water a fraction of a second before it hits water. It's actually marvelous, you know. It's written up in such a way as to predict the future. Now this has been done before; I mean it is mainly an illustration of the fact that the effect does not precede cause, I think. Have I misinterpreted the story?

Isaac Asimov (off-mike): No. Actually it wasn't a story. Actually it was a mock article entitled "The Endochronic Properties of Resublimated Thyrathymalene." What I was doing was satirizing science directly.

Miss Morgan: Now tell me this, because some friends of mine who know more science than I do have said that such a thing is possible.

Isaac Asimov (off-mike): Not as far as I know.

Miss Morgan: And I said that if that was possible, I would rather not understand anything about science and believe in spiritualism.

Isaac Asimov: Well, I'll tell you how it happened. I was working for my PhD, and as part of the experiment I was running over and over again, I was dissolving something called cadacol in water. Cadacol dissolves very quickly in water and consisted of a very fine powder—very fine flaky material anyway. And as soon as it hit the surface of the water; it was gone. Now it is very dull sitting there, doing experiments over and over again, and since I'm more than a scientist—I'm an sf writer—why naturally I had to do a little thinking. I said to myself how do you know that the material is dissolved in water when it hits the water? May be it dissolves a millimeter before it hits the water. Now ordinarly I would have promptly written an sf story based on that, but I was about to start writing my PhD thesis; therefore, I had my mind full of that, and I figured in order to purify and defuse and make it possible for me to write in the naturally cruddy style that was required why I would first make fun of it. So I did. I wrote a mock PhD thesis on that, and asked Mr. Campbell to publish it under a pseudonym, because it would come out just about the time I was up there being examined for my PhD, and I didn't want those squares getting the idea that I didn't take chemistry seriously and flunking me on that alone. Well, John Campbell, in his usual wonderful way, ran it under my name. And it came out just as I got up for my PhD examination, and one of the questions asked me was to describe the thermodynamic properties of resublimated thyrathymalene. I was unable to do so. Fortunately, there were other questions I couldn't answer either, so it didn't spoil a perfect record.

Bruce Franklin: We're forty five minutes—an hour and forty-five minutes—with the postponement—over our alloted time. So I'll give everybody here a chance for a final word. Then I hope that a lot of people here with similar interests who don't often have this opportunity can continue some of these discussions at other quarters.

Isaac Asimov: Okay. My final word will simply be about my being old-fashioned in respect to locomotives. Yes, of course, but you know these old-fashionednesses are born out of a person's whole personality. I never fly. I never take planes. If I had to be tied to the front of a conveyance, it's got to be a locomotive, because I will not be tied to the front end of a jet plane.

Darko Suvin: My final word is that locomotives are terrible in the United States. In Canada, where I happen to be at the moment, there is a beautiful new turbo train between Montreal and Quebec. There is one in France, one in Japan, on the monorail. So you see all things are relative. That's what I was trying to say in my talk, too.

Fred Pohl: My final word is that all of the things that everyone has said about sf are right.

Isaac Asimov: Man of 7,560,000 Words

Lewis Nichols / 1969

From the *New York Times Book Review*, 3 August 1969. Copyright © 1969. Reprinted by permission of the *New York Times* Syndication Sales Corporation.

Climb to the second floor of a neat, middle-class house in West Newton, Mass., bear to the right, walk a few steps and you come to a door. On it are stickers, "Great Lover," "Silence Please," "Genius at Work." Obviously in the house there are children, and, as usual, the pasted-up graffiti of children have something going for them. "Great Lover" we can skip as being nobody's business. As to the others—well, this door leads to the office of Isaac Asimov.

Silence he needs, for this definitely is a hard-working man and one of fierce concentration. Genius he may be, although he disputes it. In the matter-of-fact way in which he writes, he puts it thus: "Just say I am one of the most versatile writers in the world, and the greatest popularizer of many subjects." These range from the Bible down through history and the ramifications of science to Shakespeare, on which he's now working. The one hundredth bound result of his labors is scheduled for fall, and in Books in Print, where the type size is small indeed, the listing of various editions of his work runs a column and a half in length.

Is he the most prolific writer in the world? Says Mr. Asimov, "No, there are others, most notably Georges Simenon. But he writes only novels." The inference is clear that M. Simenon, word demon that he may be, would be hard put to turn out such an item as *An Easy Introduction to the Slide Rule*, which Mr. Asimov did. The Asimov books average 70,000 words, he has written 108 of them (the last few are still at the printers) and all this comes to 7,560,000 words. "And the most pleasant thing about it is that everything I write gets printed."

He is forty-nine, reasonably slight of build, the type of man who thought he should put on a necktie while meeting a visitor, then said the hell with it on the grounds it would be unnatural. The most distinguishing things about him are the heavy frames holding his glasses and the incredible neatness of his office. This last is as well, for he spends practically all his life there, knocking out ninety words a minute on an electric typewriter, with a back-up typewriter should the first one break down.

He leaves his typewriter unwillingly and as seldom as possible—going forth into the outer world only to give an occasional lecture or when his wife and two teenage children insist he take them somewhere. The members of the family are crosses to be borne, if pleasant crosses. "I'm really happy only when I'm up here working," he says with a wry grin.

He met his visitor at 8:30 in the morning—this unholy hour a concession to his working day—and while he talked of himself and his work he seemed on occasion to furtively eye the idle typewriter. People from New York can be as great a nuisance as a family.

His story technically begins in Russia, where he was born, but really in East New York—which is Brooklyn—where he grew up. His father operated candy stores, and indeed Isaac worked in or was otherwise connected with candy stores until he was twenty-seven, got married and withdrew. He entered Columbia at fifteen, received an A.B., kept going to an M.A., was in the armed forces, returned to Columbia for his Ph.D., and thus became entitled to call himself "Dr. Asimov."

More important to this particular story than the Ph.D. is the fact that at age eleven, he found himself with an urge to write. In a series of five-cent copybooks, he wrote eight chapters of a novel called "The Greenville Chums at College," which, it is perhaps unnecessary to say, was modeled closely on the Rover Boys. When he was sixteen, his father dipped into the somewhat lean till of the candy store to buy him a secondhand typewriter, and young Isaac was, in effect, off to the races.

This began with science fiction. At eighteen, he sent his first story to John W. Campbell, editor of *Astounding Science Fiction*. That came back, but the same editor on October 21, 1938—this date is well-remembered—bought a story called "Marooned Off Vesta," which appeared five months later in *Amazing Stories*. Mr. Asimov remembers a detail, not hard under the circumstance—he got $64 for the six-thousand four hundred word story.

In 1950, his first book, a science-fiction novel called *Pebble in the Sky*, was published by Doubleday, but a year before he had begun to take aim at fields beyond science fiction. By then, a professor of biochemistry at Boston University, he collaborated with two colleagues on a textbook which proved successful (three editions thus far) and this led him to science, minus the fiction. Finding he could explain science—well, by logical steps, he also could explain the Bible, history, what have you.

He still has one contact with Boston University. "Each year, I give the opening lecture for a course in biochemistry. No fee, of course, but a sort of introductory thing, which I try to keep light and amusing, and is attended by secretaries as well as students. I hope we all have a good time; I know that I do."

The neatness of Mr. Asimov's day is as neat as his office. The usual one—and the usual is seven each week—opens at about 7 o'clock, when he gets up, has breakfast and goes to the post office, arriving at 8 sharp, when it opens. He is what is called a "morning caller," meaning that he collects his own mail rather than waits for delivery, and the simple truth here is that he does so in order to drop junk mail in the post office's wastebasket rather than his own. On a recent day the mail he brought home consisted of the following: a publisher's contract, a royalty check from New American Library, a Canadian publisher's formal agreement to terms, contracts for inclusion of an article in an anthology (he's also one of the most thoroughly anthologized writers around), a bill, five fan letters from people saying they liked what he had written, a request for a contribution, eight magazines.

He is through with the mail between 9:30 and 10, and is ready for work. There are a thousand volumes in his personal library, 126 volumes of bound Asimov writings. The book-cases are low because of the sloping ceilings of his attic habitat, and the books are arranged as fiction, non-fiction, history, science, etc. There are filing cabinets at various places about the room, the high-speed typewriter is beside a table he uses as a desk. Should he look from the window, he would see a willow tree in the yard, but he does not look. He doesn't cut the grass, either. That would take time away from writing.

He types his ninety words a minute until about 5 o'clock, sometimes having a coffee break, and always trying not to overeat at lunch. Usually he goes back to the shop after dinner and sometimes remains there until 10 o'clock, when he takes outgoing mail to a box in front of nearby Warren Junior High School.

The comings and goings of high-school students would drive a lesser man frantic, but he doesn't hear them. Some nights he quits at 8 rather than 10, and then tries to find funny programs on TV or reads mysteries, magazines or science fiction. He'll miss the Smothers Brothers.

In the Asimov scheme of things, there is no secretary, no typist, no agent. He arranges his own indices, reads his own galleys, runs everything through the typewriter at least twice. In this modern age, everything changes fast, and when he comes on changes, from reading scientific papers and the like, he makes marginal notes in the pages of his own works—thus having a filing system that always is up-to-date. The notes become revisions for later editions, or source material for entirely new books.

Mrs. Asimov, the former Gertrude Blugerman, born in Toronto but married in 1942 in New York, keeps her part of the house as neat as he does his. Womanlike, however, she wants a vacation now and then, and the one he remembers was a couple of years ago when he gave in and they went to a hotel at Annisquam on Cape Ann. The college student personnel was arranging a parody of Cole Porter's *Kiss Me Kate* for the enjoyment of the guests, and hearing that a writer had arrived, asked Mr. Asimov to help with the lyrics. He spent seven wonderful days at a typewriter, never going outdoors. He never saw the show, either, but his wife did, reporting one guest as saying to another that the music wasn't very good, but oh, those lyrics! It was the greatest accolade he has had.

It takes a good many publishers, hardcover and paperback, to keep up with the Asimov output and its many subjects. Doubleday and Houghton, Mifflin publish about 60 percent of his work, and as he puts it, "both represent a father image." In January, the first-named father image will celebrate the twentieth anniversary of *Pebble in the Sky* by publishing *The Solar System and Back*, a collection of essays written over the last eleven years for the magazine of *Fantasy and Science Fiction*. This October, the other father image will publish *Opus 100*, this one hundredth book being an anthology of material chosen by the author from his first ninety-nine. His favorite book? "The last one I've written."

The world is the oyster for Asimov, and for the future there are vague plans for almost everything therein save two. No mysteries are on the schedule, and no books on computers. He has been asked to write his autobiography, but counters this with the remark, "What can I say?" There could be something in the future wind here, however, for he asked his father, Judah Asimov, now seventy-four and retired, to put down notes for *his* autobiography. When these come in, they are filed away and could end up as background for the Asimov younger days.

The elder Asimov also writes on a typewriter. Having bought a couple when times were tough so that his son could become a writer, he finally bought one for himself. He wouldn't accept one as a gift. Rugged individualist.

Untitled Interview from *Words and Their Masters*

Israel Shenker / 1974

From Israel Shenker, *Words and Their Masters* (Garden City, NY: Doubleday, 1974), 253–55. Copyright © 1974.

Isaac Asimov, who has taken all knowledge for his province and all book-shelves for his work, celebrated his speedwriting by arranging for five new books—including his hundredth, called *Opus 100*—to be published within a single month.

A few may have written as many, but has anyone written about as much? Dr. Asimov (whose Ph.D. thesis was on the inactivation of the enzyme tyrosinase) began as a science-fiction author, moved on to write about science, and now deals with history, theology, etymology, and literature.

When one of his publishers suggested a centenary volume in which the author would rattle on about himself, Dr. Asimov objected: "Any writer who is a monster of vanity and egocentricity—like myself for instance—would love to write a book like that." He wondered who would read it, though, and accordingly gave the publisher a word of advice: "Worry!"

A week after # 100 came # 101—*Great Ideas of Science*, and the month of Asimov wound up with volume 102—*ABC's of Space*.

It took the Stakhanovite of letters twenty years for the hundred books, thirty-two in the first ten years, sixty-eight in the next ten, with sales in the hardcover American market alone an estimated quarter of a million books annually.

"I don't indulge in scholarly depth," he said in an interview. "I don't make creative contributions. I'm a 'translator.' I can read a dozen dull books and make one interesting book out of them.

"I'm on fire to explain and happiest when it's something reasonably intricate which I can make clear step by step. It's the easiest way I can clarify things in my own mind."

He is clearest on the problems of existence: "Cities have become too large to be managed. IBM is too large to get a guy out to my house on time."

18

Dr. Asimov takes that final failure to heart, since he types his manuscripts on an IBM electric typewriter and bought a second one in case something went wrong with the first.

The first had conked out, the second was developing problems, and IBM's repair man was late. "All I get now when I call IBM is a mechanical voice," Dr. Asimov complained. "They promised to get me a man at ten o'clock. By eleven o'clock I may be dead."

His life as an author began at age eleven—when young Isaac wrote his first book ("The Greenville Chums") as a simple way to provide himself with reading. After a precocious childhood in Brooklyn and university studies at Columbia, he accepted an offer in 1949 from Boston University's School of Medicine to teach biochemistry there.

"I didn't feel impelled to tell them that I'd never had any biochemistry," he recalled. "By 1951 I was writing a textbook on biochemistry, and I finally realized the only thing I really wanted to be was a writer."

He is still on Boston's faculty for one lecture a year to the freshman class, but his keyboard is king. Dr. Asimov types ninety words a minute, reads his own galleys, does his own indexes, has an excellent memory and therefore does not bother taking notes, and reads quickly.

"I have deadlines, but I always meet them," he said. "In twenty years I haven't frozen at the typewriter. Aside from the usual biological urges, the only thing I want to do is write. If I were offered a job advising a President, or sitting on top of the Statue of Liberty, or swimming the Atlantic, I'd refuse them all."

The warm-up begins each morning as he peruses a New York morning newspaper. Believing firmly that you don't have to read it all, he rarely dips below the headlines. Then he circles another paper or two, rarely alighting, and deals with his mail—which almost always includes requests for new books, articles, and lectures.

By eight-thirty, seven days a week, he is seated at the console, testing whether his electric typewriter is made for Renaissance man. "I switched my typewriters to alternating current," he said, "so I produce two books as the current goes different ways."

One work-in-progress during his greatest month was *Asimov's Guide to Shakespeare*, which stemmed from a book called *Words of Science*. "*Science* led to *Words on the Map*," he explained, "which took me to *The Greeks*, which led me to *The Roman Empire, The Egyptians, The Near East, The Dark Ages,*

The Shaping of England, and then *Words from History.* It was an easy jump to *Words in Genesis,* which brought on *Words from the Exodus.* That led me to *Asimov's Guide to the Old Testament,* and then *The New Testament.* So what was left except Shakespeare?"

He smiled when he said that. "I grin an awful lot," he said. "But if you see a man with black-rimmed glasses and an angry look, it's me, because when I'm not smiling my face settles into belligerency."

His greatest temptation—the only one that keeps him (willingly) from the delights of alternating current is the opportunity to reread his own books. In fact, he said, "I'd almost rather read what I write than write what I read."

A Conversation with Isaac Asimov

Earl G. Ingersoll / 1976

From *Science-Fiction Studies*, vol. 14, 1987: 68–77. Copyright © 1987. Reprinted by permission of SF-TH, Inc.

When his autobiography *In Joy Still Felt* appeared in 1980, Isaac Asimov could count over two hundred books published in the three decades since his first novel, *Pebble in the Sky*, was printed. In addition he has published more stories and essays than even a man of his prodigious energy has gotten around to counting. One of them, "The Prolific Writer," which originally appeared in the October 1979 issue of *The Writer*, examines the mixed blessings of such prolificity. To be prolific, he warns, one must be a "single-minded, driven, nonstop person."

Surveying the list of Asimov's publications, one is struck by the range of his writing, from scores of books on mathematics and the sciences (he holds a Ph.D. in chemistry from Columbia) through studies of history and guides to the Bible and Shakespeare. If his name has become a household term, however, it is because of his SF: his *Foundation* trilogy, along with Arthur Clarke's *2001* and Robert Heinlein's *Stranger in a Strange Land,* is unquestionably one of the seminal works of American SF.

What follows is largely a transcript of a conversation that took place on October 20, 1976, during a visit by Asimov to the State University of New York College at Brockport. The other participants were area writers Gregory Fitz Gerald and Jack Wolf and an undergraduate student, Joshua Duberman. To their questions Robert Philmus has added one other, in his obliging response to which Asimov refers to his most recent work.

Wolf: As most of us know, you've given us the three laws of robotics. Is there a correlation between the stress on robots in your stories and your feeling, as expressed in your essays, that SF should be fundamentally a social literature? You speak often of *social* SF.

Asimov: By my own definition, SF is the branch of literature which deals with the response of human beings to changes in the level of science and technology. Over the past two centuries, we have watched our society grow more and more machine-made, so to speak; and I assume that in *one* of our possible futures, machines will continue to play more and more of a part in our society—in fact, to the point where machines may eventually "take over." So, a good portion of my stories deal with this possibility; I have machines beginning to have human intelligence and capable of doing all sorts of complex tasks we associate only with human beings; and eventually I write stories in which the machinery does, more or less, threaten to take over.

My own feeling is twofold. In the first place, I don't feel robots are monsters that will destroy their creators, because I assume the people who build robots will also know enough to build safeguards into them. Secondly, when the time comes that robots—machinery in general—are sufficiently intelligent to replace us, I think they should. We have had many cases in the course of human evolution, and the vast evolution of life before that, in which one species replaced another, because the replacing species was in one way or another more efficient than the species replaced. I don't think *Homo sapiens* possesses any divine right to the top rung. If something is better than we are, then let it take the top rung. As a matter of fact, my feeling is that we are doing such a miserable job in preserving the Earth and its life-forms that I can't help but feel the sooner we're replaced the better for all other forms of life.

Wolf: Maybe we won't leave much that anything except robots could live in.
Asimov: Give us thirty years, and the replacement will come too late.

Duberman: In your robot stories and in your *Foundation* trilogy, you outline a possible future that has been taken over by other SF authors, perhaps because your view is more efficient.
Asimov: As a matter of fact, we authors in SF are more or less friends; we inhabit a small, specialized world in which we are comfortable, and the general feeling is that ideas are common property: if one SF writer thinks up something which is very useful, another may put it into his own words and use it freely. Nobody in SF is going to accuse any other person in SF of using his ideas; in fact, we borrow so generously that there's no way of telling whose idea it was originally. For instance, in my novel *The Caves of Steel*, it was very important to the plot to have moving sidewalks, with an elaborate

system of side strips that enabled you to work up to the speed of the sidewalk or to work down to the surrounding, motionless medium. This had already appeared some years before in Heinlein's "The Roads Must Roll." Well, I borrowed it without any worry at all. I'm sure that Heinlein in reading my novel would have recognized his system, but who knows where he got it from? He never said anything. It'd be different if I used the details of his plot, if I worked up a story that was so like his that nobody could fail to see it— that's plagiarism. But just to use the idea and build your own plot or story about it—why, we do that all the time. And they do it from me, too—you know, they use the three laws of robotics—and they're welcome. I have no objection.

Fitz Gerald: To return to what you said earlier about mankind being replaced, Charles Elkins has said that your work expresses the view that human nature doesn't change. Is that a fair representation of your judgment?
Asimov: Some people have pointed that out in my *Foundation* trilogy, which takes place tens of thousands of years in the future. Although there is some evolution of science, there is no evolution in human behavior, and there is a reverse evolution in political science; in other words, we go back to a kind of feudalism.

Fitz Gerald: That's why I ask that question: to see how you rationalize technology's and science's lack of effect upon human nature itself. In other words, don't you suppose that with dynamic changes in technology and science, human nature itself will be changed also?
Asimov: Well, it's possible, but that was not my purpose in writing the *Foundation*. I wanted to consider essentially the science of psychohistory, something I made up myself. It was, in a sense, the struggle between free will and determinism. On the other hand, I wanted to do a story on the analogy of *The Decline and Fall of the Roman Empire*, but on the much larger scale of the galaxy. To do that, I took over the aura of the Roman Empire and wrote it very large. The social system, then, is very much like the Roman imperial system, but that was just my skeleton.

At the time I started these stories, I was taking physical chemistry at school, and I knew that because the individual molecules of a gas move quite erratically and randomly, nobody can predict the direction of motion of a single molecule at any particular time. The randomness of their motion works out to the point where you can predict the total behavior of the gas very accurately, using the gas laws. I knew that if you decrease the volume, the pressure goes up; if you raise the temperature, the pressure goes up, and the volume expands. We know these things even though we don't know how individual molecules behave.

It seemed to me that if we did have a galactic empire, there would be so many human beings—quintillions of them—that perhaps you might be able to predict very accurately how societies would behave, even though you couldn't predict how individuals composing those societies would behave. So, against the background of the Roman Empire written large, I invented the science of psychohistory. Throughout the entire trilogy, then, there are the opposing forces of individual desire and that dead hand of social inevitability.

Fitz Gerald: Would it be accurate to say, then, that for you the laws of history are as inexorable as the laws of physics?
Asimov: Well, I wanted them to be for this particular story. I could easily write another story in which I would take the attitude that the laws of history are not in the least inexorable. This is a very important thing to remember. It's very tempting to suppose that the point made in a story is something the author believes. This is often so, but it is not always necessarily so. Frequently an author thinks of a motif which has the advantage of being interesting, exciting, dramatic, but which he doesn't personally accept. For the sake of the story, he'll put it in. For instance, I wrote dozens of robot stories, all designed to show that we need not have the Frankenstein complex: the robots are protected by the three laws, human beings know that they're in no danger, etc. When someone asked me to write what I considered the ultimate robot story, I decided the only way I could make it "ultimate" was to get around the three laws of robotics and produce the Frankenstein motif again. So I did. The title of the story was "That Thou Art Mindful of Him." I wrote that story, and anyone reading it would assume I believed robots would end up a danger to human beings. In fact, I got a number of indignant letters from fans, saying how could I possibly bring up the Frankenstein motif when I'd spent so many years denouncing it.

Wolf: Did you get any letters from robots?
Asimov: [*Laughter*] No, the robots were satisfied with my job. But my only answer to those fans was: I thought up a dramatic story, and I wasn't going to allow my own beliefs to get in the way.

Wolf: One of the charges levelled against SF projection is that it assumes the laws we have discovered, those operable on Earth, are of necessity the same ones that operate throughout the galaxy or universe, and that this is not necessarily the case.

Asimov: Well, scientists know that this is not necessarily the case, and they keep looking for evidence that it is not, but so far they haven't found it. And SF writers have sometimes assumed that the laws are different and based stories on that, but generally they don't because it gets complicated. My novel *The Gods Themselves* dealt with two universes in which the laws of nature were different; I just made a slight change in one law of nature and tried to work out the consequences. It's not easy! Almost any assumption can be violated in SF, on the condition that you know what the assumption is and that you know you are breaking it and can let the reader know that you know. Unfortunately, in many cases, people who write SF violate the laws of nature, not because they want to make a point but because they don't know what the laws of nature are. This always shows, and it makes the SF inferior.

Wolf: Sometimes it's hard to be certain exactly what the law of nature is.

Asimov: That's why it's better to have some background in science, not necessarily a formal one; you can work up a background on your own. People forget that the great revolutionaries of science *knew* thoroughly what they were revolutionizing. In other words, Galileo knew Aristotelian physics. Vesalius knew Galenic anatomy, and Newton understood all the theories of the universe. No one has revolutionized science by not knowing what came before. Many people who write me letters with brand-new theories of the universe haven't the foggiest idea what the present theories are. And you just can't do it that way.

Wolf: Somewhat off this topic, but you mentioned that if robots are in a position to take over some time in the future, so be it. This reminds me of Sam Moskowitz, who in *Seekers of Tomorrow* speaks of the classic debate—back in 1938, I think—between you and Donald Wollheim: in case of invasion, should the Earth surrender to a superior civilization? As I recall, your position was that the Earthmen should fight against this surrender.

Asimov: All opinions have to be considered in the light of the times: 1938 was the year of Munich, and when they asked, "Should we surrender to the invading civilization?," it was impossible not to think of surrender to the Nazis simply because it looked as though they were more powerful and they were going to win. At that time I said, "No, you have to fight to the death," because surrender was going to be a lot worse than fighting to the death—you're better off dead, or at least I would have been, since I was Jewish. And that reflected itself in my position. Obviously times change, and now that thermonuclear war might conceivably destroy mankind generally I can't accept the better-dead-than-Red argument. I'm perfectly willing to have the better-dead-than-Red argument on an individual basis—if you'd rather die than give in to the Communists, fine! But is it wise to kill the entire human race rather than to give in to Communism? There, you figure, if you give in, you might in some future generation win out again. For the entire human race to be dead is final. At different times in my life, I might give different answers to the same question.

Wolf: I see now, and I wouldn't dwell on it any longer, but we need to add that we wouldn't have been giving in to a *superior* civilization, had we given in to the Nazis.

Duberman: *The Gods Themselves* was your first SF novel in a long time. Throughout the '60s you were producing magazine articles and books by which people could further their knowledge of science. Why did you stop, and why did you start writing SF again?

Asimov: In the first place I never really stopped writing SF altogether; I would always turn out a small story or two every once in a while. I didn't write any SF novels because I got interested in writing other things, and an SF novel is a very time-consuming thing. I don't think I can write an SF novel in less than seven months, and in those seven months, even when I'm not typing, I'm thinking about the novel a lot. Whereas, if I write non-fiction, it goes very quickly, I don't get involved with endless thinking, and I can turn out a book a month. That's fun, for me. I like to be typing, I like to be turning out books; I don't like to stay awake nights thinking that maybe I ought to change the plot to include this or that—you know, it gets very difficult. SF is the most difficult thing there is to write, and I'm essentially a lazy person, so I like to write other things when I can. Even mysteries are easier to write. My mystery novel *Murder at the ABA* was written in seven weeks. I couldn't for the life of me write an SF novel in seven weeks! I just couldn't!

Fitz Gerald: Could you be more specific about why, other than the amount of time, SF is so much harder to write?

Asimov: Oh! That's very easy. In SF there are two aspects: first, there is plot, the complications of events; that's the same as in a mystery novel; but, secondly, you have to build a new society, if you want to write a good SF story. This society, if you do it properly, should be just as interesting as the plot itself; in other words, the reader should be just as eager to read about the society and to picture it as to see the development of the plot. But you don't want to subordinate one to the other: you don't want the plot to be so intricate and so dense that you can never see the background through it; on the other hand, you don't want the background to become so prominent that you lose sight of the plot taking place in front of it. In the end, therefore, you have to maintain this perfect balance, as I think I maintain it, for instance, in *The Caves of Steel*. It's hard to work it out. You have to do a lot of thinking and writing and rewriting, whereas in mysteries you're using the present society. When you're writing non-fiction, of course, you don't even have a plot.

Fitz Gerald: Is it fair to generalize, then, that for you the powers of invention are taxed more fully in SF than in other forms?
Asimov: Yes, provided it's good SF. Bad SF is easy to write. If you really try to turn out a piece of good SF, it just takes everything you've got in you. At least in my case, it does. In the case of *The Gods Themselves*, I started out to write a 5,000-word short story, and it got away from me.

Duberman: The style of that novel seems significantly different from that of your earlier work, especially the characterization and the idea of an alternate world. Was that the first time you approached that?
Asimov: Well, I rarely deal with extraterrestrial beings in my stories; some thought because I couldn't handle it. I suppose that did irritate me a little; so when I wrote *The Gods Themselves*, I deliberately placed the middle third in another universe and worked up a set of extraterrestrials which were not just humanoid creatures, not just human beings with antennae, but *really* completely different in every possible respect. I tried so hard to show them that I could do it that I turned out what I think—and some people would agree—is the best story of extraterrestrials ever written.

Also, my novels and stories never contain explicit sex and very rarely contain romance; my explanation, when someone asks, is that I'm a pure person, at least in my fictional life. This they tend to disbelieve and say that I just don't have the capacity to deal with sex, so in the other universe of

The Gods Themselves I had that section of the plot completely involved with sex—every line of it, so the plot made no sense without sex and all its details. Of course, it was extraterrestrial sex and, therefore, nothing like ours; but that's all right.

Wolf: I'd like to ask another question about the *Foundation* series and your approach to psychohistory. Much of that, at least theoretically, reminds me of the current "think tanks," the Hudson Institute and others. Did you have any of that in mind?

Asimov: No, because the essence of the Foundation appeared in a series of eight stories in *Astounding Science Fiction*. The whole notion of psychohistory appeared in the very first story, which appeared in the June 1942 *Astounding*; it was written in 1941, when I was twenty-one years old. That was well before "think tanks," and I had no knowledge of them when I wrote it.

Philmus: Virtually all readers who have made their thoughts about your *Foundation* books public have pretty much attended exclusively to what you yourself emphasize: the notion of psychohistory operative in them. Yet it seems to me that a quite different, and counterbalancing, conception also informs the original trilogy, at least. You've just reminded us that the earliest stories in your trilogy came out at about the same time as, say, *The Hamlet* and "The Bear"; and it seems to me that those stories of Faulkner's have a certain kinship with yours. What I mean is that your stories, too, appear to belong to the American tradition of the tall tale, featuring as they do the adventures and exploits of individuals of legendary proportions. I therefore wonder to what extent you conceived of them as such, and also to what extent your subsequent, and exclusive, stress on the psychohistorical—i.e., impersonal—forces at work in them is the result of your being influenced by your interpreters.

Asimov: You must understand that of all the successful writers I am probably the least well-read. As a youngster, I read indiscriminately at the local library—which meant, for the most part, nineteenth-century fiction and twentieth-century non-fiction. By the time I grew old enough to move into twentieth-century fiction, it was too late: I was too busy writing to read anything but material directly related to what I was writing. This admission is in order to explain that I have never read one word that Faulkner has written—right down to this day. I don't advance this as either praiseworthy or blameworthy, but merely to indicate that I have never been influenced by him directly. It is conceivable that I have been influenced by someone who was influenced by Faulkner, but I have no way of telling that.

As for psychohistory versus the "tall story." . . . While I have larger-than-life heroes, that is just because pulp fiction always did (The Shadow, Doc Savage, etc.—I read them and *was* influenced by *them*). That, however, was not what I was interested in. I was interested in psychohistory from the very start, and I was careful to show that when heroes had psychohistory on their side, they won; when they did not, they lost.

Of course, my fascination with psychohistory altered with the decades. By the 1980s, I had come to the decision that psychohistory would get nowhere if human ways of thought, human social systems, etc. did not change fundamentally. Beginning with *Foundation's Edge*, psychohistory as a tool was de-emphasized and I began to consider fundamentally different social systems—that of the first Foundation, that of the second Foundation, that of Gaia. I continued this in my two robot novels of the 1980s, *The Robots of Dawn* and *Robots and Empire*. And I continue it still further in my latest book, *Foundation and Earth*.

Fitz Gerald: I'd like to ask you a question about SF as literature. You have written during the period of greatest change in SF. What projection would you make about the direction in which SF is going now?

Asimov: SF is the only branch of fictional literature that is flourishing. In general, fiction is in the doldrums, certainly compared to what it was when I first came into the field. In those days there were literally dozens upon dozens of "pulp" magazines; there were "slicks" that published fiction; there were all sorts of literary quarterlies; and publishers were eager to put out novels. The beginning writer had plenty of places to go. Nowadays the "pulps" are gone; the "slicks" that are left don't publish fiction; there are no literary quarterlies; publishers don't like to publish fiction, especially first novels. As a result, young people who want to write are in a quandary. Since SF alone is flourishing, a lot of them are writing SF, with the result that there is a certain dilution of SF. It's becoming more literary, more experimental in style, less *science* fiction, because a lot of the writers don't happen to be full of expertise in science. They don't think they ought to be; they don't think we ought to have *science* fiction, but *speculative* fiction in which you speculate about the future in any style you happen to like. And I suppose they're right. In the future, as long as we have a future, SF will broaden, become more dilute, and spread out until it overlaps all of fiction. I think all people who write fiction are going to have to take into account certain SF trends, especially that society is changing faster and faster. Within this broad field of SF, there will be a narrower field of old-fashioned SF, dealing entirely with scientists and science. I'll still be in that narrower field.

Wolf: You're very careful in your essay on social SF to specify that you're talking not about the term *science* generally but something like technology. It seems to me that's what you're talking about here, because fields we now identify as sciences—psychology, psychoanalysis, sociology—do not lead to technologies. Obviously, if you're talking about SF in those terms, you're going to get a much broader definition.

Asimov: Yes, but in the *Foundation* trilogy I deliberately and specifically dealt with what we might call political science or the science of history, and developed a technology for it. That was my attempt to broaden the notion of science in SF. On the other hand, we have extremely gifted writers like Harlan Ellison, who couldn't be less interested in science; he concentrates entirely on human beings and does it very effectively. It's only SF by courtesy, and he recognizes that. He's in the forefront of the movement to use the term "speculative fiction." His forerunner in the field was Ray Bradbury, who also knew no science and didn't want to. Ray's stories have great poetic value.

Wolf: And he doesn't consider himself an SF writer.

Asimov: No, he doesn't. He's a fantasy writer; I called him at one point a *social* fiction writer, and he accepted that at the time.

Wolf: Probably *Fahrenheit 451* is as technological as most of what passes for SF.

Fitz Gerald: But it's not very extrapolative.

Asimov: No, it's very hard to make these hard-and-fast boundaries. Everything fades into everything else.

Fitz Gerald: To what extent do you think "hard SF" is a preparation for books like *Future Shock*?

Asimov: I tend to agree with Toffler. It's difficult not to, and be human. I don't like change that upsets my well-worn way of life, but I do know that change *will* take place. I may not like it, but I'm not outraged. As a matter of fact, what we might call the "SF attitude"—"hard SF"—is essential if we are to survive as a technological society. Unfortunately, too many people just take it for granted that things won't change or that if they do they shouldn't, and you should make every effort to restore the status quo. As a result, we're not prepared for the changes, and we make no effort to direct them in optimum fashion. We're going to be overwhelmed in a couple of generations by the changes that are now taking place, most of which are undesirable. Unless we can look these changes boldly in the face, try to figure out what we ought to do to prevent these undesirable changes and to bring about desirable ones, to think hard about distinctions between desirable and undesirable ones, we are certainly going to go under. Now, no matter what we do, we may go under, but I would prefer to do something which would give us a chance than do nothing, which would give us no chance at all.

Fitz Gerald: You produced for us the three laws of robotics, but how about coming up with three laws for human beings so that when we manufacture human beings by means of genetic engineering we can have the built-in protections you gave us for robots.
Asimov: That's an interesting thought, which I've never considered. Well, why don't I think about it? I'd hate to come up with something off the top of my head, because it wouldn't be as good as if I were to give it some thought, and because I might like to write a story about it.

Fitz Gerald: You wouldn't mind if I wrote one about it, too?
Asimov: Oh, no! [*Laughter*] By all means. It's your idea I'm stealing, right?
Fitz Gerald: No, we're sharing.

Wolf: What you were talking about earlier has been taken up by Susan Sontag, among others, who says that the imagination of disaster in SF makes us too ready for change. We grow indifferent to the moral concepts involved, and we figure that change is inevitable so it doesn't matter particularly what the change is. The result is that out of complacency or becoming inured to the inevitability of change, we abrogate our feeling of being able to control our futures, and we go along with what's given to us.
Asimov: I don't accept that as a proper interpretation of the attitude of SF. SF does not simply talk about change as an abstract thing. Every SF story

describes a certain, particular change and decides whether it's for the better or the worse. Generally in SF stories the change is for the worse, or threatens to be for the worse, *not* because SF writers are essentially pessimistic, *not* because change is essentially for the worse, but only because this makes for a more dramatic story. If you write a story about a change which produces human happiness, you come out with a *Looking Backward* that Edward Bellamy wrote, which is an interesting book but a dreadful story—it's very dull. So we are constantly writing anti-utopias, the idea being that this is a change we don't want to take place; how do we prevent it? In the story frequently the villain is defeated, change is aborted, something better seems to be on the horizon, a threatened change for the worse is prevented and so on. SF teaches that there are numerous changes and that mankind by its actions can pick and choose among them. We should choose one which is for the better. *That* is the proper interpretation of the role of SF.

Wolf: Although we're becoming a more and more technological society and we have more scientifically oriented people around, we're getting less scientifically-oriented SF. Doesn't that seem paradoxical?
Asimov: Not really. Partly it's a disillusionment with science; partly it's because we're getting a lot of hard-core SF in the newspapers and magazines. Landing *Viking* on Mars is hard-core SF; what we wrote about for years is now being done. Also, as I said earlier, many people who are now writing SF are doing so in default of anything else and aren't interested in science.

Wolf: Are you moving away from SF because you're disillusioned with it as a viable form of literature?
Asimov: No, I think it's extremely viable. I will admit that I feel a little ill at ease with modern trends in SF—the highly stylistic, emotion-saturated SF of today. The decreasing percentage of hard-core SF makes me feel like a back number.

Wolf: Any number of times the charge has been levelled that SF is fundamentally cerebral, rather than emotional, and therefore character isn't developed in SF, with all the ramifications involved. The current trend is not only away from character but also away from that cerebral side, and toward action.
Asimov: Yes, it is. When I described earlier in this conversation the difficulties of balancing background and plot, I meant also that spending time on

background takes time away from your characters. You don't have characterization as it's usually understood by most people. If you consider your background society as a character, that society has all kinds of "characterization,"
but that's not usually considered so by critics. On the other hand, now that
writers are trying to remove the cerebral quality and to add to the emotional,
to work with characterization in the older sense, they do it at the cost of the
background. In many modern SF stories, you have people very sharply delin-
eated, but you see a society only by flashes of lightning. There is no such
thing as a free lunch: if you gain something here, you lose something there.

An Interview with Isaac Asimov

James Gunn / 1979

Done in preparation for writing Isaac Asimov: The Foundations of Science Fiction (Oxford, 1982). Reprinted by permission of James Gunn.

In April of 1979, upon the occasion of the Nebula Award weekend, I visited New York to interview Isaac Asimov in preparation for the writing of *Isaac Asimov: The Foundations of Science Fiction*, which was published by Oxford University Press in 1982—an expanded version, including Asimov's post-1982 best-sellers, will be published by Scarecrow Press. He took an hour away from his guest duties at a New York City science-fiction convention, held at a mid-town college or university, as I recall, and we had the following conversation in a large, otherwise deserted, downstairs lobby.

Gunn: When you write about your own writing you seem to be asking: how did it come to be so successful?
Asimov: Yes, you're perfectly right. To this day I don't know the steps by which it happened. The success of writers such as Bob Heinlein and Van Vogt seemed easy to understand because from their first stories they were recognized as extremely good science-fiction writers, whereas I don't think in the case of my own first few stories there was any thought on the part of anybody, including myself, that I was a particularly good writer. I was a new writer and no one paid much attention to me. Even when "Nightfall" appeared, it didn't seem to me that it made much of a difference because it appeared in the same issue with stories by Heinlein that completely drowned it out.

Gunn: Throughout *The Early Asimov* and the other collections in which you added autobiographical notes as well as in the first volume of your autobiography, what makes all this concentration on Asimov and his writing tolerable is a note of delighted surprise that it ever came out that way?
Asimov: Yes, I'm still delighted, and I'm still surprised.

34

Gunn: The question keeps coming up: how did it happen? And that's one thing I'm going to be writing about in my book about your science-fiction writing. I'm interested in treating your work as being not only the unique product of your own personality but also a kind of expression of what science fiction was at the time, in the sense that what you wrote encapsulates what science fiction was concerned with.

Asimov: In a way, I suppose, I was the perfect foil for John Campbell. On the one hand I was close to him. I lived right in town and I could see him every week. And, for another, I could endure him. That is, I imagine that a great many other writers found him too rich for their blood—at least to sit there and listen to him hour after hour. But I was fortunate in the sense that he was in some ways a lot like my father. (Laughter) And I had grown up listening to my father pontificate in much the same way that John did, and so I was quite at home. I suppose if you took all the time that I sat there listening to John and put it together, it was easily a week's worth of just listening to him talk. Day and night. One hundred and sixty-eight hours. And I remembered everything he said and how he thought and I did my best—because I desperately wanted to sell stories to him—to incorporate his method of thinking into my stories, which, of course, also had my method of thinking, with the result that somehow I caught the Campbell flavor.

Gunn: That's close to what I wrote in the third volume of *The Road to Science Fiction*. Each of the stories is preceded by biographical notes, and I commented about you, and I hope you don't feel it denigrating, that you were the quintessential Campbell writer. You were Campbell's kind of writer; whereas Heinlein, I felt, was always his own kind of writer who just happened for awhile to write things that coincided with what Campbell wanted.

Asimov: I think you're right. I think you're right. Certainly towards the end, Campbell would say things to me that led me to think that, too.

Gunn: Well, one thing I wrote was that the over-riding element of your fiction (there are a few places where it doesn't quite fit) is the search for answers—the application of reason, rationality, to complex, puzzling situations. There is very little of the triumph of emotion over rationality. Or if it does, it is a kind of tragic circumstance. It is a happy circumstance when reason triumphs over emotion, or when people find a solution to whatever it is that bothers them.

Asimov: You're right; you leave me nothing to say, because I agree with you completely there.

Gunn: As a matter of fact in the third volume of *Road to Science Fiction* I reprinted the story "Reason." Like you I delight in puns and I called the biographical headnote "The Clear, Cool Voice of Asimov."

I have read virtually all the science fiction you have ever published. I wonder whether the reason the stories in *The Early Asimov* were not included in your other anthologies was that they were in some way inferior—they didn't live up to your vision of what they might have been. It seemed to me that at some point you discovered that you liked to incorporate in your stories an element of mystery and suspense. I wondered whether you would feel it to be a fair statement that when your stories began to really incorporate not just detective elements, but always a kind of mystery to be discovered, this was really when your fiction began to please you, and began to be successful in your own eyes.

Asimov: Well, now that's very interesting, because I think perhaps you're right. Certainly the first stories that really satisfied me and made me feel good about my writing were my robot stories, and the robot stories, of course, virtually every one of them, had a situation in which robots—which couldn't go wrong—*did* go wrong. And we had to find out what had gone wrong, how to correct it—within the absolute limits of the three laws. This was just the sort of thing I loved to do. And I enjoyed it.

Gunn: And so when you began to write mysteries—science-fiction stories as mysteries—it was really nothing new because you had really being doing this all along with the robot stories, except they weren't presented as detective stories—there was no formal detective, but Susan Calvin was doing the job of a detective.

Asimov: Yes, that's right. And then by the time I got to *The Caves of Steel*, there was a robot story in which the detective element was formal. And I did the same with *The Naked Sun* and then it was just natural progression to go to straight mysteries. Which I now enjoy more than I do science fiction—it is as though I've discovered what I really like and I can do that even without the science fiction. And, incidentally, this is very old-fashioned. People don't do it anymore—even the mysteries, the straight mysteries I write—are extremely old-fashioned and I suspect that if I weren't me I couldn't sell them. And this is another thing that constantly puzzles me about my own writing and I hate to talk about it too much for fear that someone else will see that. But to put it as briefly as I can—how do I get away with it? Because, when I wrote *Murder at the ABA*, for instance, even on the book jacket, it said "an old-fashioned mystery" and I thought, gee, there's the kiss of death. Who's going to read an old-fashioned mystery? Well, enough people read it so that it was reasonably successful. And now my autobiography is, if ever I saw one, an old-fashioned autobiography, because there are no sexual revelations in it—there are no deep psychological probings. I don't have any sensational revelations whatsoever. It's just the ordinary story of an ordinary life and yet it's doing fairly well.

Gunn: Maybe it's because you have an insight into publishing some publishers don't have, that people have always been willing to read old-fashioned works. There may be a basic kind of appeal there that the publishers are overlooking.

Asimov: Well, that could be. In any case, fortunately, my publishers are very pleasant to me and usually let me have my way, in sort of a very fatherly way. You know that's another place where I have been extremely fortunate. Campbell took what I consider to have been a fatherly interest in me. He had a number of writers who came to visit him periodically or corresponded with him and discussed with them in those late '30s and early '40s—that first five years in which he was editor, which were the most creative of all. And I think that of all the writers I was the youngest, in years, and still young in outlook. I was naive, unsophisticated, and therefore somehow he felt that I was most malleable, the most easily molded, and he enjoyed molding me, so to speak. And he was in loco parentis—he was a father in almost everything but the literal sense of the word, and literally he was a father. And this somehow has been the same attitude that, to a somewhat lesser extent, all my editors, virtually all, have since taken to me, even when, as in recent years, they've turned out to be, say, twenty years younger than I was. Right now my Doubleday editor is a young woman named Kathleen Jordan, who is approximately a quarter-century younger than I am. And yet her attitude toward me is distinctly motherly. I have the feeling—in fact it is not something I really had to dig for, because it's quite open and obvious on the surface—that she's out there making sure that I don't fall over my own big feet, you know, and she won't let me do things that I shouldn't, because she says no, I'm not going to let you, Isaac, and I know she worries about me. So, I suppose I could say that by the most peculiar coincidence something like a dozen editors with whom I've been close in books and magazines have all just happened to be the fatherly—the parental—type. But I don't think that that is conceivable. I think that rather what it is that for some darn reason I inspire this in other people, I think largely because I am quite obviously naive and unsophisticated. (Laughter) I don't really think that I am, but that's how I must impress others.

Gunn: To get back for a moment to this question about the mysteries, it seems to me as I look over the stories that there are a couple of basic ways in which one can deal with characters in a story. They can either have a problem to solve or else they themselves can change and in your stories, few of your characters change—you talked about that in your 1953 essay "Social Science Fiction," that people are pretty much the same, they don't change, the circumstances change. And of them all, I can only think of one Asimov story where a person changes and that's probably "The Ugly Little Boy." This is probably one of the few stories—there may be one or two others—which might be called "stories of character." And I wonder whether you ever felt that or ever were aware of the fact that one could deal with stories of character, even within science fiction—or thought of it in those terms?
Asimov: Well, I knew that it could be done. I also knew well that it might be too difficult for me to do. I don't know that I have the kind of literary power that is required for that sort of thing. I can deal with rational action, but I'm not sure that I can deal with the inner recesses of being. Now "The Ugly Little Boy" was something I had written on a dare. No one had made it to me, I made it to myself. I got tired of having people tell me that I had no women in my stories. That's true, I rarely have women in my stories, and that's a matter of choice—I'm not at ease with women in my stories, largely because I started writing long before I'd had so much as a date with a girl. Women were strangers and aliens to me and I never quite got over that. Even though in real life they are no longer strangers and aliens. But I got tired of hearing people say that, and so, to show myself, I decided to write a story in which a woman was the chief character, but not a woman like Susan Calvin, who is rationality personified, but a woman with emotions. So I sat down to do that, and that's what came out. It's not necessarily what I planned—it just worked itself out that way. It's one of the few stories I've written that routinely makes

women cry. At least I've received phone calls and letters from people saying that they've read "The Ugly Little Boy" and it made them cry at the end and invariably I answer and say I am pleased because it made me cry when I wrote it—which it did. The only other story I've ever written in which I felt that I was deliberately, more or less, reaching for the pocket handkerchief at the end was "The Bicentennial Man," where that, too—although I didn't plan it!—is a story of character because Andrew, the robot, develops all the way through. He not only forces recognition of himself as a man—that is the external change—but all through internally he becomes more and more of a man. So, there again I did it. So, I suppose I can do it. I can do it, but I don't necessarily tend to, because what I concentrate on mostly is the problem.

Gunn: The puzzle, the mystery?
Asimov: Yes.

Gunn: You've often said that you don't know much about writing and I wonder, if I may say so, if this isn't a pose, a bit disingenuous? (Asimov laughing) Because clearly you have thought about it and you've attended the Bread Loaf Conference and they must have talked about things which I'm sure did not go over your head. And you've mentioned the incident in which you noticed how Clifford Simak left gaps in his stories to indicate a change of place or action. First you thought that was offensive and then you realized that this was a good thing to do and so you learned how to do it yourself. You have picked up things and I just wonder whether you think a little bit more about this than your public pose would suggest.
Asimov: Well, now, that's really hard to say. I swear to you that I don't deliberately set up a pose—it's what I tend to think. There was a book recently called *Isaac Asimov*—a collection of essays about me—edited by Martin Greenberg and Joseph Olander, and I wrote an appendix called "Asimov on Asimov" in which I first denied that it was at all possible—that I could possibly have inserted all that meaning in my stories, and then I presented the opposite view that maybe I could, at that, without even knowing it. So that it's possible that consciously I don't think much about the mechanics of writing. I don't sit down and brood about it or try to think it out or discuss it with people, but that without very much in the way of conscious thinking I manage to learn from what I read and from what I hear. For instance, I remember distinctly reading once that you have written that it is necessary to

engage several of the senses. And whenever I can remember, I try to do so, you see? But it's very difficult for me to remember in the fury of composition.

Gunn: The first time I learned that I put the five senses up in front of my typewriter so that I would be reminded. (Laughter) Carolyn Gordon taught me that a number of years ago. In Donald Wollheim's book *The Universe Makers*, he speculates that psychohistory is the science that Marxism pretended to be and I wondered whether you ever consciously thought about that in that relationship.

Asimov: Well . . . you know that's so difficult to answer because psychohistory originated in a discussion between myself and Campbell, as so many of the things in my early science-fiction stories did. And I think Campbell must have been reading about symbolic logic at the time. There is some reference to symbolic logic in the first story and that was more or less forced on me by John Campbell; it didn't come naturally to me, because I knew nothing about symbolic logic. And he felt in our discussion that symbolic logic, further developed, would so clear up the mysteries of the human mind as to leave human actions predictable. The reason human beings are so unpredictable was we didn't really know what they were saying and thinking because language is generally used obscurely. So what we needed was something that would unobscure the language and leave everything clear. Well, this *I* didn't believe, so I made it mathematical and *my* analogy was, of course to the kinetic theory of gases, where the individual molecules in the gas remain as unpredictable as ever, but the average action is completely predictable, so that what we needed were two things, a lot of people, which the galactic empire supplied and secondly, people not knowing what the conclusions were as to the future so that they could continue to act randomly. And that's the way it worked out. Now, when Wollheim says that it was what Marxism pretended to be, well when Wollheim was young he was very interested in Marxism and undoubtedly read a lot about it. I've never read anything about it, you see, so it's a case of his reading his bent into me. For me, it was the kinetic theory of gases and that was secondarily imposed and it was John Campbell who really started it with symbolic logic.

Gunn: At that time you may not have been aware of H. G. Wells's talk to the Sociological Society in which he said that a true science of sociology was

impossible because there aren't enough people involved to make accurate prediction possible.
Asimov: No, this is the first I heard of it.

Gunn: You weren't aware of it?
Asimov: No, not until now I haven't been aware of it. (Laughter)

Gunn: There is a kind of parallel in that obviously—I say obviously, it is obvious now—obviously in the Foundation stories you supplied enough people so that the laws of physics can be applied to those numbers. H. G. Wells said there weren't enough people to apply these kinds of laws to, so he suggested that sociology really ought to be concerned with a kind of setting down of utopian visions of the future and sociologists would then criticize them and judge whether they would work. As a matter of fact there is another parallel your autobiography brings out: Wells wrote in his autobiography that he was very much at home in biology because he took his first year at the Normal School of Science under T. H. Huxley. It was a shaping experience for him. His second year I believe was in chemistry, and it was OK, but he didn't have as good a teacher and his studies went downhill. His third year was in geology and was a total loss, and physics he knew nothing at all about, and of course he was great at history as you are. And almost the same kinds of parallels, it seems to me, were evident in your own interests in your college educational career. You have indicated that the higher mathematics stumped you eventually when you got up to the upper reaches of calculus and physics was not really your field.
Asimov: No.

Gunn: I wondered if there is some similarity, not in the careers themselves, but simply in the kinds of minds that were involved.
Asimov: Well, since I'm a great admirer of H. G. Wells, I find this funny. (Laughter)

Gunn: To go back to *The Foundation Trilogy*, I am curious—at what point in the whole series did the concept of the Second Foundation occur?
Asimov: Well, from the very start—

Gunn: Right from the first conversations with Campbell?
Asimov: Right, because I remember Campbell saying we'll need two Foundations.

Gunn: Because it's never mentioned in the First Foundation series—it's mentioned in the introductory story that you wrote for the Gnome Press edition, but as I recall, and I could be wrong, I didn't see any mention of a Second Foundation until we get into the second volume.
Asimov: Well, it's my impression, and I swear, I can't say for sure, that in the very first story, "Foundation," there was a casual mention of the Second Foundation, because it was there from the beginning. [Asimov was right.—J. G.] I did not know what the function of the Second Foundation was to be. It was there as a safety measure, as a reserve, as a strategic reserve, in case something developed in the plot so that I needed a way out, that would be the Second Foundation. And as a matter of fact, it became necessary once we introduced the Mule. Now the Mule was introduced by Campbell over my virtually dead body—which was in a sense a good thing—it was one of the many occasions in which Campbell was right and I was wrong and I never try to hide those occasions. He wanted to upset the plan and I thought that was heresy. He said to me—don't worry, think of all the fun you'll have trying to get it back on track. And so I remember distinctly saying to myself, well if he's going to make me destroy the plan, the only way I could get back at him was to write the longest story I had written up to that time, and I did, I wrote fifty thousand words. I'd never written a fifty thousand-word story before and he was glad to pay for it. Of course, it was the best piece; it was the best thing in *The Foundation Trilogy*.

Gunn: You make the comment in your autobiography that he made you change the ending of "Now You See It," the sequel to "The Mule."
Asimov: Yes.

Gunn: To permit the continuation of the series. But you don't say what your ending was.
Asimov: I don't remember—I don't remember.

Gunn: Oh, I see. . . . (Laughter) You don't remember how you were going to end it. Maybe the Mule wins out—maybe he was going to find the Second Foundation?

Asimov: No, no—I was going to reveal what the Second Foundation was and have the Second Foundation triumphant as it was, but reveal where it was and no more. But I don't remember where I had said it was, that's the point, and Campbell made me take it out, because he wasn't going to let me finish, and then I wrote one more and after that nothing on earth could have made me continue, it just got too heavy.

Gunn: Yet, in many ways the last book, *Second Foundation*, may be liked better by a lot of people because of the character of the girl.

Asimov: Yes, yes, Arkady, she was good. It was the only time I ever tried extended treatment of a teenage girl and I enjoyed that very much. It was not that I couldn't write more about the Foundation, it was that the situation under which I wrote it, individual stories in magazines in which each one had to be self-contained—where you have to assume that it was quite possible that somebody was going to start reading it that hadn't read any of the other Foundation stories—you had to explain everything that went before—it just got so hard. Now if I had written it in novel form, so that instead of having eight stories of different length I had three novels as a trilogy, I could undoubtedly have had a fourth one.

Gunn: It wouldn't have been as difficult.

Asimov: Yes. But in those days, there were no novels, no books. Everything appeared in magazines.

Gunn: This is one thing I want to deal with in my book, the influence of the medium of communication on the things that were not written—they obviously influenced what was written.

Asimov: Well, yes. Another thing was it was ephemeral. In other words, you expected a story to appear in a magazine and be there for a month, and then be gone forever, except for those who collected the magazines, and well, you know, that meant you were paid once for it. In fact, there was no concept of subsidiary sales. Never heard of such a thing. You sold a story, you got some money for it, a penny a word or whatever, and that was it, forever. So that the emphasis was writing it fast, on trying not to have to revise, because you wanted to write more and make more money. If you were trying to make a living. That was what enforced pulp writing, which is essentially first-draft writing and sure-fire writing. It gave the stories a lot of action. When you write nowadays, even for the magazines, you know there are going to be anthologizations, there are going to be collections and so on. You can afford to take your time and do a little better, because you know that there's going to be considerably more money involved than just that initial sale.

Gunn: In my own case I am convinced that the harder I work on something the more successful it eventually is. That isn't universal in all cases, but it generally pays off today to do as good a job of writing as you can, irrespective of how long it takes.
Asimov: Um-hum.

Gunn: To get back to the fact that the mystery may be your mode of writing fiction, perhaps this develops rather naturally from the fact that your writing generally shows the triumph of reason or the struggle of reason to triumph over various kinds of circumstances including emotional reactions to situations that are existing. So that, if this is true, if reason is going to eventually emerge triumphant, the mystery is the natural form in which it will be exercised. Does that make sense to you?
Asimov: Yes, it does.

Gunn: The solution to problems is the way in which reason demonstrates its desirability.
Asimov: Yes, it does make sense. And it reminds me that my villains generally are as rational as my heroes. In other words, it's not even a triumph of rationality over irrationality or over emotion, at least not in my favorite stories. It's generally the conflict between rationalities and the superior winning. The good guys, so to speak. In other words, if it were a western where everything depended upon the draw of the gun, then it would be very unsatisfactory if the hero shot down a person who didn't know how to shoot. In fact . . .

Gunn: It has to be an equal balance.
Asimov: That's right, where the measure of superiority is very small, where there is some question as to whether the hero will win. And occasionally, very occasionally, I have the side win in whom I don't believe, in other words there

is a story I wrote called . . . oh, hell, what's the story called? . . . "In a Good Cause," that's it. . . . "In a Good Cause," where the person who at the very end wins out is the person whom I consider the villain. What happened was that as I wrote the story, the winding paths of rationality made him win out against my will. (Laughter) Doesn't often happen; generally I'm in better control and the side I favor wins.

Gunn: It seems to me also that your fact articles, your science articles, are often written the same way your fiction is. You present a mystery. How did this happen; how did somebody come to this conclusion? And then you show the reason it worked out that way, again, almost as if it were a mystery story.
Asimov: Well, now, I'm glad you said that, because this is not something I have myself spent time thinking of, but I think you're right now that you present it. The way I almost invariably explain anything is historically. I start at the beginning and carefully describe how various people have added elements of knowledge to a particular problem and the way I explain it to myself is that it's important people understand how a problem is solved and exactly the way it was indeed solved, rather than have them think that scientific knowledge is something handed down from Sinai. Furthermore, the easiest way of making sense out of it is to follow the path of what actually happened, because you follow that path along the line of gradual elimination, and there is probably no alternate path that is as illuminating. But that invariably means the unspoken question is—how was this discovered? How was this problem solved? And, in fact, in the essay I have most recently written, which is about the neutrino emissions by the sun, I start off saying that I always begin at the beginning and this sometimes annoys my editors—but I have written a book on the neutrino in which before I ever said a word about the neutrino I carefully described how the concept of natural laws of conservation were worked out, the significance of it, the apparent violation of no less than three of those laws. The necessity of inventing a particle that could save all three of those laws, and the fact that you could save all three with a single particle, is a very strong suggestion that that particle did in fact exist. And it wasn't until the book was exactly half over that I got to the point where I introduced the particle. And so chapter seven was entitled "Enter the Neutrino." And Walter Bradbury wrote in the margin "at last." And yet I wouldn't have dreamed of doing it any other way, because it would have spoiled the suspense. In fact, as I said in my autobiography, my dissertation

was spoiled for me, absolutely spoiled for me, because my professor insisted I explain what the symbol M stood for, despite the fact that I told him it would spoil the suspense.

Gunn: To go back for a minute to psychohistory, I noticed something in your autobiography that perhaps you may or may not have been aware of—the fact that there was a great deal of commentary, kind of footnoted commentary, which suggests a belief in determinism. You make continual references to the fact that as the boy was, so is the man, that, "I was imprinted by this at an early age," "because I had to eat hurriedly as a youngster, now I still eat hurriedly," "because I did things that way then, I do them this way now"—I wonder if you feel that that's an explanation in a sense as to why psychohistory became a congenial notion with which you could deal—whether the fact that this notion of early determinism fits in with the notion of psychohistory.

Asimov: Well, I'm trying to think now, you see, I was only twenty-one when I started writing the Foundation stories and then I had the general notion in my head, and I didn't change that general notion. Now at the time I was twenty-one I had not had time to notice, I think, that I had developed habits that dated back to an early age. Now I'm old enough to see that there isn't a reason in the world why I have to eat fast. But, no, I don't think that's why—I'll have to go back to what I said before. When I was twenty-one, I was doing graduate school, I had taken physical chemistry—physical chemistry was important to me, because I had to pass it with a B in order to stay in school. More than any other course I ever took, that one sort of hovered over me with its fangs and claws extended, so that I worked harder on that course than any other course I'd ever taken. And one of the things that particularly impressed me was the careful working out of the laws of gases. Partly because, I suppose, it was so difficult for me to understand, but I got it firmly fixed in my head that you arrive at certainty through uncertainty. That even though every atom or molecule thinks it has a free will, it doesn't, because on the whole it doesn't, and mind you, this was also at a time when I'd been living through the Hitler era in the 1930s, where no matter what anyone did, Hitler kept winning victories, and the only way that I could possibly find life bearable at the time was to convince myself that no matter what he did, he was doomed to defeat in the end. That he couldn't win.

Gunn: Psychohistory is against it.

Asimov: That's right. And as a matter of fact, we started with the Foundation bound to win, no matter what the forces arrayed against it. I suppose that that was my literary response to my own feelings, which have no basis, I suppose, except that it made me feel better. To the inevitable victory of the anti-Nazi causes, although they seemed to be steadily losing. And, you know, the first two stories of *The Foundation Trilogy* were written in 1941, which was just about Hitler's peak. They were published in 1942. I think that might be the way it worked out.

Gunn: In the last portion of *Second Foundation* there is a kind of ambivalent attitude toward the Second Foundation, that the psychologists are going to establish eventually a new kind of society in which mental science is going to be more important than physical science and in essence are going to be the new rulers. And that seems to me to be not a great idea! (Laughter)

Asimov: What my thoughts were as I was writing it—you see whenever I wrote a Foundation story I didn't spend too much time thinking about what the next ones would be, but on the other hand, I didn't want to write anything that would make it impossible to write any more, because I was interested in keeping the series going.

Gunn: Even though you were determined to end it with *Second Foundation*.

Asimov: Nevertheless, in case I ever wanted to continue, I needed sufficient ambiguity so that I could write more stories. I honestly wasn't sure as I wrote *Second Foundation* how the Second Foundation was going to be different from the Mule; the Mule was ruling, so to speak, by mental science, and the Second Foundation would be ruled by mental science. Wouldn't the Second Foundation be sort of Mule by committee?

Gunn: There is this element in it I think and I suppose there was a possibility of writing a sequel in which some kind of more democratic force overcomes the coercive and elitist Second Foundation.

Asimov: Well, that was exactly the sort of dim thought I had—that in the end, by God, it was going to be the First Foundation that would triumph even over the Second Foundation.

Gunn: Well—(laughter)
Asimov: I hadn't the faintest idea how that would work, but I was sure that was what was going to happen.

Gunn: Some criticism attempts to deal with *The Foundation Trilogy* as if it were conceived and written in one flash of inspiration or one continuous effort. It seems to me that this is misguided, that one has to assume that this was written piece by piece and the only reasonable criticism is one which assumes that you solve this problem and then later you come back and you say, now where do I go, and put another problem on top of that which I can solve, and so rather than dealing with the *Trilogy* as a kind of total mental exercise, it represents a kind of exercise in ingenuity.
Asimov: You're perfectly right. In fact I've been planning to write, under extreme pressure, another Foundation novel and I even wrote eight pages, and this time it is going to be a novel and not a series of short pieces—it's going to be a full-length novel, unitary, and I was going to have my characters searching for the Second Foundation. Now the people in the First Foundation do not know it was the Second Foundation which saved them. The whole purpose of the Second Foundation was to remain under-cover, to not let people know—as soon as people know the Second Foundation is taking care of them, the very equations the Second Foundation uses lose their validity. And yet we have one character who is convinced that the Second Foundation does exist and is going to search but it is going to take an entire novel. I imagine I can do it, but I also have this horrible feeling that I'm no longer in my twenties, that *The Foundation Trilogy* was co-terminus with my twenties. I started writing the stories at the age of twenty-one and I finished it at the age of twenty-nine. And now I can write much more skill-fully than I could then. I am technically more proficient, but I also somehow lack some of that energy, you know? And I'm going to end up with a book which reads much more smoothly and somehow grabs people much less, I'm sure.

Gunn: You are going to do it?
Asimov: Well, if I ever get around to it, but I dread it. I really dread it. I fear, I fear people saying, "*The Foundation Trilogy* is great, but don't read that fourth volume." (Laughter)

Gunn: Let me get to a particular point of a particular story that seems anomalous—in "Green Patches."
Asimov: Yes.

Gunn: If I read it correctly, the story talks about the little multipliers in the darkness, which apparently are bacteria, green-patch bacteria—the attempt to solve the problem has failed. And I wondered—that's one of the few cases, I think—if that reading is correct—where reason and the exercise of common caution and so forth, fails in one of your stories. Is that a correct reading?
Asimov: Well, you know, I don't remember. The only thing I remember about that story is that I was demoralized in the middle. I had gotten halfway through and I suddenly realized that I was writing an infinitely inferior— what was the name of John's story that I liked so much?—oh, "Who Goes There?"—I was writing an infinitely inferior "Who Goes There?" And I was halfway through it when I realized it and I called up John and I said what I was writing and I said, John, it's just like your story "Who Goes There?" Oh, well I said, Mr. Campbell—now I say "John," but in those days I always said "Mr. Campbell," to the very end. And he never said, he never said, call me "John," either. He always called me "Asimov"—not "Mr. Asimov," just "Asimov." Anyway—

Gunn: Proper teacher and student relationship.
Asimov: Right. Absolutely, absolutely. Now I say "John," and when I think back, I always describe myself as saying "John" (laughter) but I never said that. As a matter of fact my college professor, Dr. Dawson, whom I always called "Dr. Dawson"—I was there at a luncheon celebrating his retirement and I'm his most prominent pupil, and I finally could bring myself to say "Charlie," always with a little hesitation. (Laughter) Anyway, I called up Campbell and told him about this, and he said, "Oh, don't worry about it, Asimov, you go right ahead; no two stories are exactly the same when a competent writer writes them." So I went ahead, but it was with a broken spirit.

Gunn: And then of course eventually it was sold to Galaxy, wasn't it?
Asimov: Yes, it was. But I don't know what I originally intended to do—all I know is that when I got to the middle point, I tried desperately to make it as unlike "Who Goes There?" as possible, and probably would have abandoned

the story, but it had been ordered by Gold. He had asked me to write a story for his first issue and I did "Darwinian Poolroom," which is a very poor story, and he took it, because he had to have a story for that first issue, there was a hole that had to be filled. And I felt very guilty, because I knew it was a poor story, and so he said, would you write me another one, and I was determined to write this other one, no matter what. And then my heart broke in the middle when I realized what I was doing, but I had to keep on writing anyway, instead of tearing it up. And so I don't remember what I had originally planned, but it's a very atypical story.

Gunn: But the little multipliers in the darkness were supposed to be bacteria?
Asimov: Well, not necessarily, they could be anything. They can infect bacteria, but they can also infect human beings.

Gunn: Well, green patches certainly could, but I was wondering about the meaning.
Asimov: Oh, I see what you mean. You're talking about the significance.

Gunn: At the end you comment about the "little multipliers in the darkness. . . ."
Asimov: I forgot that. . . .

Gunn: I presume that the creature that was destroyed nevertheless had stimulated within human bodies bacteria, the creation of bacteria, which were products of the green patches, and now although it had been wiped out, the people were going to go ahead on to earth carrying the seeds of their destruction, and probably the destruction of life on Earth, within their bodies.
Asimov: Do you know . . . that's completely, I swear I never thought of that—I'll have the reread the story myself.

Gunn: I was wondering, now, what was it you meant by little multipliers in the darkness?
Asimov: I don't know, I'll have to reread the story. Oh my goodness, I didn't even recognize the phrase, frankly. When you said little multipliers in darkness I didn't know you were quoting me.

Gunn: Yes, it was a direct quote and the phrase is ambiguous and it's kind of strange, because I think most of your stories do not carry that kind of ambiguity, I mean that kind of coyness about naming names. I wasn't sure exactly what. . . .

Asimov: Well, I'll reread the story and then I'll write you on that. [He never did, and the ambiguity remains.—J. G.]

Gunn: In his book, Joseph Patrouch wrote that you have not written about what you are most concerned about—that is pollution, overpopulation and so forth—in your fiction—but it seems to me that you show people living with these problems and solving them in your fiction. In *The Caves of Steel* there is the problem of overpopulation, but it's something the people are living with—people are adaptable. But it seems to me that in talks and in your science articles you exhibit a kind of an alarm about our public position, about our situation—what I call your public despair as contrasted to your fictional optimism.

Asimov: Yes, that's because in my public statements I have to deal with the world as it is—which is a world in which irrationality is predominant; whereas in my fiction I create a world, and in my world, my created worlds, things are rational. Even the villains, the supposed villains are villainous for rational reasons.

Gunn: The way I put it is this: that in your science writing you try to persuade by showing the terrible consequences of what is likely to happen, and in your fiction you try to persuade by showing how people can solve their problems.

Asimov: OK.

Gunn: Finally, I think we're getting close to the end. At least I sense in your autobiographical writings of all kinds a great deal of what I might call a high level of loyalty to what you were; to the boy you were and to what science fiction was when you discovered it. That is unlike what has happened to some other writers, who have gone on and put away what they once were. Like Harlan Ellison, for instance, who may say, well, that's all past, it's not me any longer, I now am off doing my own thing. A perfectly reasonable attitude, but the opposite is what you display. I think a lot of people feel that this kind of loyalty makes you different and maybe admirable. But I wonder whether you ever felt that science fiction is not as important as it was.

Asimov: It's not as important to me, personally. I write comparatively little science fiction. But, Jim, this is a matter of deliberateness on my part. In many respects I frequently say I follow the line of least resistance. I don't deliberately try to write well, I just write as it comes, and if it happens to be good, thank goodness, that sort of stuff. But as far as this business of not abandoning my origins, that's deliberate. I made up my mind when I was quite young—and I said it in print in places—that no matter whatever happened to me, no matter where I went, I would never deny my origins as a science-fiction writer and I would never break my connection to science fiction and I never have. I attend every convention that I can reach. Unfortunately, I don't travel much, so I can't reach many of them, but I attend every one. I never accept any money, not even for car fare, not even when it is out of town. I'll talk at every one, as I did today, and I never try to deny that I'm a science-fiction writer, even when I am writing very little science fiction. I identify myself as a science-fiction writer, and so on. Now, why do I do this? In the first place, because I consider loyalty one of the prime virtues. When we started my magazine I wouldn't give up my *F & SF* articles, for instance, and I forced Joel Davis to accept that as a condition. And I probably bore everybody with my endless repetition of how much I owe to John Campbell, because I would rather bore them than be disloyal in my own mind. It is the easiest thing in the world to forget the ladder you climb or to be embarrassed at the thought that there was a time when somebody had to help you. And the tendency is to minimize this, minimize that, and I suppose I'm normal enough and human enough to do the same thing if it were left to itself, but this is a matter of having once made a vow and I stick to it. It's inconvenient to always have to tell people that Campbell made up the three laws of robotics, and the more important the three laws become the more I want to be the originator and take the credit, but I can't. Now, as to why this is so, I never really thought about it. I guess I like to think about it only as a matter of virtue. I don't consider myself a particularly virtuous person, but I like to think I have some virtues, of which loyalty is one. But possibly it is because I am not a very good Jew. I don't attend any Jewish religious functions, I don't follow any of the Jewish rituals, or its dietary laws, or anything about it, and yet never under any circumstances do I leave any doubt at all that I'm Jewish. I really dislike Judaism. I'm against it—it's a form of particularly pernicious nationalism in my opinion. I don't want humanity divided up into these little groups that are firmly convinced each one that it is better than the others, and Judaism is the prototype of the "I'm better than you" group—we were the ones who invented this business of the only God. It's not just that we have our God and you have your God—it's that we have the only God and you've got something less, you know? And I feel a deep and abiding historic guilt about that. And every once in a while when I'm not careful I think that the reason Jews have been persecuted as much as they have has been to punish them for having invented this pernicious doctrine. And so, I suppose, because I feel that in some ways I have been a traitor to Judaism, which I try to make up for by making sure that everybody knows I'm a Jew, so while I'm deprived of the benefits of being part of a group, you know, I make sure that I don't lose any of the disadvantages, because no one should think that I am denying my Judaism in order to gain certain advantages. But in order to make up for that, I made up my mind that I'm not going to be disloyal in any other way, and there it is, I suppose. I'm not saying I believe this, but this is the sort of thing that people do work up for reasons, and, after all, I'm imaginative enough to think up such reasons, too. So if you want one, there's one handed to you free of charge, but I don't guarantee it's correct.

Gunn: If I were seeking an explanation—I don't want to embarrass you by giving you descriptions of yourself as I've been trying to do, there seems to me to be a kind of common element among science-fiction readers and science-fiction writers—that is a kind of disturbed puberty, or a disturbed adolescence, one which finds itself uneasy socially and there is a kind of displaced sexual activity which goes into reading and a desire to write and the whole thing, which I think one finds among many science-fiction writers, myself among them, a kind of emphasis more on reason and intellectual abilities, perhaps to make up for the fact that most science-fiction writers have problems fitting in. I think Damon Knight said that all science-fiction writers and fans start out as toads. But that is a preface. I wonder whether you could accept that you see yourself as a person who is trying to live a life of reason in an emotional world. A world where reason is not that much valued and that certain conflicts arise out of this.
Asimov: Well, first I'll have to admit, you can see for yourself in my autobiography, that I had a great deal of difficulty adjusting to the world when I was young, and to a large extent the world was an enemy world, and Robert Silverburg, who read my autobiography, has written me saying he can't wait for the second volume and he wants the galleys. Because he says there is so

much in my life that parallels his own, that it gives him a feeling of déjà vu to read it. And I suspect that what you have said and what Knight has said is not only true of science-fiction writers, and to a lesser extent of science-fiction readers, but obviously true. It is science fiction and its very nature is intended to appeal a) to people who value reason and b) to people who form a small minority in a world which doesn't value reason. And science fiction is that kind of an escape. Now, I am trying to lead a world of reason in an emotional world. For instance, I have just recently—*Reader's Digest* asked me to see a person who claims he has a way of breaking up water into hydrogen and oxygen and then burning it and solving the energy problems of the world—and I listened and I said it's impossible—it's a perpetual-motion machine, it goes against the Second Law of Thermodynamics, and he told me it's not. And I said there is no reason to argue about it. If you will make it work I will cheerfully admit I'm wrong. And to my way of thinking, this is my feeling. Here is a person who I can clearly see is in a sense irrational, or at least he supports something which cannot be supported by rationality. I oppose that with what I consider a rational statement. He denies it, why argue? Since it is irrational, it's not going to work. When it does work, we'll talk about it. In a way, it's a way of retreating from something that is too painful to immerse yourself in fully. I once received a postcard from someone who said what would you do—this was after an argument about Velikovsky—what would you do if some scientific discovery tomorrow proved that Velikovsky was correct? I replied, saying in that case I would cheerfully accept Velikovskyism and admit I had been wrong. I would also go skating in hell, which by that time will have frozen over.

Gunn: You mention in many places that you have a remarkable memory. From one who does not have a very good memory—do you have any clues as to how your memory works? Not how you got it, but was it just something that you know how it operates or is it something that is sheer magic and simply comes up with what you want to know?
Asimov: It has to be sheer magic. Talking to somebody about when people realized that sound was a wave phenomenon, I said that I thought it couldn't be before somebody had worked up a system in which they would spread sand over a flat surface, a flat, level surface, and then draw a bow, a fiddle bow along one end of it and set it to vibrating, so that the sand would be thrown off the parts that vibrated—and you get interesting little symmetrical

patterns and that made it clear, at least as I remember, that sound was a wave phenomenon. Now what bothered me at the time is that I couldn't remember, and invariably I go into a kind of panic when that happens.

[This is where the battery ran out and the rest is too faint for transcription. But I recall that Asimov went on to say that his memory almost always supplies the information he needs, so that when it doesn't he feels the kind of panic he expressed here. And he mentioned an occasion when he was addressing a group of Gilbert and Sullivan enthusiasts and for a moment couldn't recall a line of one of the lyrics and panicked, and then the line came to him and he went on. He didn't think anyone else noticed, but he thought—this is what most people must feel most of the time.—James Gunn]

The Plowboy Interview: Isaac Asimov—Science, Technology . . . and Space!

Pat Stone / 1980

From *Mother Earth News* 65 (September/October 1980). Copyright © 1980.
Reprinted by permission of Ogden Publications, Inc.

Isaac Asimov is one of the world's most famous science fiction authors. His *I, Robot* and *Foundation* books are regarded as classics in the field . . . and his short story "Nightfall" was once proclaimed—by its creator's colleagues—the greatest science-fiction story of all time!

Dr. Asimov is *also* respected for his ability to write about scientific subjects for the general public. He's composed over a hundred such books, on every topic from photosynthesis to the collapsing-universe theory. And, in addition, the incredibly prolific author has penned mysteries, annotated guides to literature and the Bible, a two-volume autobiography *(In Memory Yet Green* and *In Joy Still Felt),* collections of limericks, and dozens of books about history. In fact, on the day that Mother visited Dr. Asimov in his New York City apartment, the writer received an advance copy of his *217th* published book!

Still, Isaac Asimov's name is not generally associated with alternative technology, self-sufficiency, ecology, or most other "Mother-type" topics . . . so some of you may be wondering why we chose him to be the subject of this issue's Plowboy Interview. (Actually, the famed author seemed a bit puzzled by the idea himself. He responded to our initial invitation by gruffly suggesting that our magazine "berates technology" and would try to cure the miseries of the world "by lynching the nearest engineer"!)

The truth is that the folks here at Mother realize it isn't necessary to agree with everything a person says in order to learn from that individual. On the contrary, it's often possible to profit *more* by listening to the opinions of a differently oriented thinker than by paying attention only to those of someone whose ideas exactly mirror our own! Furthermore, humanity's future *will* be inexorably linked with the problems and potentials of science and technology . . . and we were sure that Asimov—whom astronomer Carl Sagan once called "the great explainer of our [technological] age"—would be bound to have some instructive and original thoughts about the role of science in this rapidly changing world.

Well, let us tell you right now that Dr. Asimov didn't disappoint us. Oh, it took a while to persuade him to agree to an interview—and he *did* seem less than enthusiastic when staff writer Pat Stone and photographer Steve Keull first arrived at his door last June—but, once everyone sat down to talk, the renowned writer treated Mother's emissaries to a very stimulating two-hour discussion.

What follows is the edited transcript of that conversation.

Plowboy: Dr. Asimov, in your science books and articles—be they concerned with black holes or biology—you always begin by tracing the development of humankind's knowledge in the subject area. Could you start this interview by giving us a bit of information about your own "historical development"?
Asimov: Gee, I don't know that there's anything particularly fascinating about my background. My family migrated, from a small village in Russia to New York City, when I was three years old. We lived in Brooklyn, my parents ran a candy store, and I worked in the store—whenever I could—during my childhood years.

Now my father thought that most of the publications he carried in his shop's newsstand were "junk," so he wouldn't let me read them. He *did* let me read science fiction, though. He couldn't speak English very well, you see . . . and I think he felt that science fiction must have had something to do with science, and that it therefore would be good for me.

So at age nine I began reading science fiction. And, over the years, I became so interested in such stories that—by the time I reached seventeen years of age—I started trying to write some of my own. My first few attempts were rejected by the magazines, but—after several months of trying—I did manage to sell some of my work.

I didn't think I could ever earn a *living* as a science-fiction writer, however, so I continued my career. I went on to enter graduate school and began studying biochemistry—and eventually became an honest-to-God scientist. I also got married, served a stint in the Army, had two children, and all the while continued writing science fiction on the side.

Plowboy: When did you make the switch from writing mostly science fiction to producing science texts?

Asimov: That phase of my career started when I was teaching at Boston University's medical school and was asked to help two of my co-workers write a biochemistry textbook. I agreed to give them a hand, and soon discovered that writing nonfiction was even more fun than writing fiction. I *also* found, however, that working with other people put limits on me, so I decided to go it on my own . . . and learned that I *greatly* enjoyed writing about science when I could do it myself *and* in my own way.

Then, in 1957, *Sputnik One* was put into orbit, and many people felt that the United States educational system had been neglecting science. So, being reasonably patriotic, I felt I ought to write more books about science, and—roughly from that moment on—my literary output became largely nonfiction.

Plowboy: Do you still write science fiction?
Asimov: Some. Actually, I now write more *mysteries.* Still, to the end of my days I'll probably be known as a science fiction writer. And I have no objection to that . . . that's the field in which I made my reputation.

Plowboy: Can you give me a good definition of science fiction?
Asimov: Every science fiction writer defines it differently. For instance, John Campbell—the great, late editor—said that science fiction stories are those that science fiction editors buy.

Plowboy: But what is your *own* definition?
Asimov: I think science fiction is the very *relevant* branch of literature that deals with human response to changes in the level of science and technology. And such writing goes to the heart of matters that trouble us now, because the world is changing at whirlwind speed. Moreover, any person who is, let us say, between fifteen and thirty years of age today is likely to live well into the twenty-first century. The world is going to be completely different then!

Now you may think that's a pretty *obvious* truth, but it isn't at all! Very *few* people realize that change is inevitable and that it will occur more and more rapidly as time goes on. So it's absolutely essential to consider the future in making our decisions . . . and to *face* that future with daring and guts.

I believe no amount of reading in any field *but* science fiction is going to convince anyone of the inevitability of change. When a person reads science fiction, though, he or she *starts out* assuming—in the story at least—that the future *will* be different.

Plowboy: So science fiction helps one adjust to the fact that the world is going to be continually changing. But such writing doesn't usually try to give an *accurate* picture of what that world will be like, does it?

Asimov: I don't know of any science-fiction writer who really attempts to be a prophet. Such authors accomplish their tasks *not* by being correct in their predictions, necessarily, but merely by hammering home—in story after story—the notion that life *is* going to be different.

Plowboy: And, as you see it, the keys to such world changes will be advances in science and technology.

Asimov: Science fiction always bases its future visions on changes in the levels of science and technology. And the reason for that consistency is simply that—in reality—all *other* changes throughout history have been irrelevant and trivial. For example, what difference did it make to the people of the ancient world that Alexander the Great conquered the Persian Empire? Obviously, that event made some difference to a lot of *individuals.* But if you look at humanity in general, you'll see that life went on pretty much as it had before the conquest.

On the other hand, consider the changes that were made in people's daily lives by the development of agriculture or the mariner's compass . . . and by the invention of gunpowder or printing. Better yet, look at *recent* history and ask yourself, "What difference would it have made if Hitler had won World War II?" Of course, such a victory would have made a *great* difference to many people. It would have resulted in much horror, anguish, and pain. I myself would probably not have survived.

But Hitler would have *died* eventually, and the *effects* of his victory would gradually have washed out and become insignificant—in terms of *real* change—when compared to such advances as the actual working out of nuclear power, the advent of television, or the invention of the jet plane.

Plowboy: You truly feel that *all* the major changes in history have been caused by science and technology?

Asimov: Those that have proved permanent—the ones that affected every facet of life and made certain that mankind could never go back again—were always brought about by science and technology. In fact, the same twin "movers" were even behind the other, "solely" historical, changes. Why, for instance, did Martin Luther succeed, whereas other important rebels against the medieval church—like John Huss—failed? Well, Luther was successful because printing had been developed by the time he advanced his cause. So his good earthy writings were put into pamphlets and spread so far and wide that the church officials couldn't have stopped the Protestant Reformation . . . even if they had burned Luther at the stake.

Plowboy: Today the world is changing faster than it has at any other time in history. Do you then feel that science—and scientists—are especially important now?

Asimov: I *do* think so, and as a result it's my opinion that anyone who can possibly introduce science to the nonscientist should do so. After all, we don't want scientists to become a priesthood. We don't want society's technological thinkers to know something that nobody else knows— to "bring down the law from Mt. Sinai"—because such a situation would lead to fear of science and scientists. And fear, as you know, can be dangerous.

Plowboy: But scientific knowledge is becoming so incredibly vast and specialized these days that it's difficult for *any* individual to keep up with it all.

Asimov: Well, I don't expect everybody to be a scientist or to understand every new development. After all, there are very few Americans who know enough about football to be a referee or to call the plays . . . but many, many people understand the sport well enough to follow the game. It's not important that the average citizen understand science so completely that he or she could actually become involved in research . . . but it *is* very important that people be able to "follow the game" well enough to have some intelligent opinions on policy.

Every subject of worldwide importance—each question upon which the life and death of humanity depends—involves science, and people are not going to be able to exercise their democratic right to direct government policy in such areas if they don't understand what the decisions are all about.

Plowboy: Are you implying that science and technology can solve all our problems?

Asimov: I think technology *can* save us, *if* it's used properly. I don't know for sure . . . some of our problems *may* prove insoluble even for science and technology. But if those two tools fail us, nothing else will succeed.

Of course, the decisions that have to be made concerning the *uses* of science and technology are not easy ones. We must consider the dangers that go along with using specific technologies, *and* the dangers that could result from failure to use them. To give a specific example, let's suppose that nuclear fission power plants proliferate. If accidents worse than Three Mile Island occur, there could be many deaths. On the other hand, if we were to close down the nuclear power plants and then not succeed in finding adequate replacements for our energy needs, there could also be many deaths. And when a person dies, it makes little difference to that individual whether he or she dies at the hands of nuclear fission or of a nuclear fission power *shortage*.

We *don't* have to decide which course of action will destroy us all or save us all, because the questions that await us aren't that simple. Instead, we have to decide which course of action has the best chance of allowing us to progress from this year to next year—and from this century to the next—with a maximum of safety. Nowhere is there a black and white dichotomy. Nowhere are the choices simple and clear.

Indeed, we're not likely to survive without *some* damage, no matter what direction we take.

Plowboy: In your opinion, what are mankind's prospects for the near future?

Asimov: To tell the truth, I don't think the odds are very good that we *can* solve our immediate problems. I think the chances that civilization will survive more than another thirty years—that it will still be flourishing in 2010— are less than 50 percent.

Plowboy: What sort of disaster do you foresee?

Asimov: I imagine that as population continues to increase—and as the available resources *decrease*—there will be less energy and food, so we'll all enter a stage of scrounging. The average person's only concerns will be where he or she can get the next meal, the next cigarette, the next means of transportation. In such a universal scramble, the Earth will be just plain *desolated*, because everyone will be striving merely to survive . . . regardless of the cost to the environment. Put it this way: if I have to choose between saving myself and saving a tree, I'm going to choose *me*.

Terrorism will also become a way of life in a world marked by severe shortages. Finally, some government will be bound to decide that the only way to get what its people need is to destroy another nation and take *its* goods . . . by pushing the nuclear button.

And this absolute chaos is *going* to develop—even if *nobody* wants nuclear war and even if *everybody* sincerely wants peace and social justice—if the number of mouths to feed continues to grow. Nothing will be able to stand up against the pressure of the whole of humankind simply trying to stay alive!

Plowboy: How can we cope with this massive problem?
Asimov: I think we'll need some sort of world government. Yet we're not even beginning to move toward such unity today. On the contrary, as I look around the world, it seems to me that even our individual *nations* are becoming less powerful than before.

Plowboy: How can that be? The atomic bomb gives many such countries enough power to devastate the world.
Asimov: Yes, nations with nuclear bombs can destroy the world . . . but they *can't* win any wars. We didn't use such explosives in Vietnam, and the Soviet Union isn't using them in Afghanistan, because the bombs are simply *too* powerful.

It may well be that—by creating a world in which terrorists can have almost all the advantages of advanced technology—science has now made any person capable of defying any government, and is thus helping to make governments feeble.

And, far from welcoming this weakening of government, I think we should realize that it's helping to *destroy* us. I would much rather see international cooperation become widespread enough to give us at least the *equivalent* of a world government.

A global ruling system could result in tyranny, of course. But a world dictatorship, no matter how distasteful, may be necessary if we're to face our problems and solve them. Conversely, the *lack* of a world government may mean global disorder and confusion . . . and I don't think chaos can solve anything.

Plowboy: What events could possibly motivate the peoples of our divided world to pull together?
Asimov: Several human characteristics could become catalysts in establishing a world government. Perhaps the most basic is *fear* . . . fear that the *alternative* to banding together could be total destruction. For example, it was such a fear that caused Great Britain and the United States to form an alliance with the Soviet Union, against Germany, during World War II.

Now I'm not asking that all nations love one another. All I hope for is that the different countries will *cooperate*. Of course, if nations work together long enough, people may eventually forget their hatred.

Plowboy: What else could lead separate countries to unite?
Asimov: We can always count on greed. It may well become necessary to build enormous structures—either on the surface of the earth or in space—to supply the world with energy . . . solar collectors, perhaps, so huge that no single country could manage to construct them on its own. And if it were to come about that feuding nations could get adequate energy supplies only by joining forces, they'd be likely to put aside their differences and cooperate out of greed.

Believe me, the obstacles that keep us from working together today are just going to melt away when energy sources are at stake! Look, for instance, at the Palestinian Liberation Organization. When Israel became a nation in 1948, *nobody* worried about the Palestinians. But in 1948 it had not yet been established that the Middle East is swimming on an ocean of oil. Now that fact *is* known . . . and the PLO can get the support of almost every country in the world. This turnaround occurred, of course, *despite* the fact that Europe is Christian, while the Middle East is Moslem, and—for centuries—there has been a traditional conflict between adherents of the two religions.

There's also a third factor that may help bring the world together: pride. If we are faced with the need to build huge structures in space to collect energy, it could prove to be a sufficiently large and global challenge—since I honestly don't think that the United States or the Soviet Union could accomplish such a goal alone or even in combination—that *all* people would want to be involved with it. Nations would *insist* on not being cut out of the project.

And it's just possible that there might be sufficient pride in the undertaking to allow people to think of themselves as citizens of Earth rather than as members of this or that subsection. We live in an era when there is a great deal to be ashamed of and a great deal to be angry about but not much to be proud of. It strikes me that the effort to truly develop space could give all people—*and* all nations—an opportunity to earn a little self-pride.

Plowboy: Trying to industrialize space would be a massive undertaking. What possible gains—other than pride and unity—could justify such an effort?
Asimov: Well, if people become sufficiently afraid of nuclear fission, and if coal turns out to be just as dangerous in a different way, and if oil begins to disappear, and if we don't manage to develop nuclear fusion or it doesn't turn out to be a cure-all, *and* if other forms of energy are just insufficient for our needs . . . then people may turn to solar energy. But in order to run our industrial world, we'd have to produce solar electricity on a huge scale, and my feeling is that this cannot be accomplished on the surface of the Earth. For one thing, the development of *terrestrial* solar power would associate energy with geography, because certain areas get more sunshine than do others.

However, we *could* collect solar energy in nearby space. A wide bank of solar cells placed in synchronous orbit above Earth's equator could collect much more energy—and do so much more efficiently—than could collectors located on the planetary surface. The electricity formed in such space stations would then be converted to microwave radiation, beamed down to receiving stations, and *reconverted* to electricity. Such energy would ideally belong to the entire population of Earth . . . instead of becoming the territorial possession of any one nation.

We could also set up orbiting industrial plants to make use of the vacuum, zero gravity, and high- and low-temperature characteristics of space. Risky work with hard radiation and genetics could be carried out "off planet," and we could spill pollution—such pollution as we can't avoid producing—into space . . . where the solar wind would sweep it beyond the asteroids.

There's yet another advantage to developing space. In order to get the job done—and to achieve global stability—we'd have to tax the richer nations *more* than they would get back and the poorer nations *less* than they would get back. Such an arrangement would correct a historical injustice, because the wealthy nations have—for a long time now—been running international corporations in such a way that the richer lands benefit at the expense of the poorer ones.

Plowboy: So your solution to our present problems is based on humankind's *continuing* to expand its territories?
Asimov: Always, always. All through history, humanity has stretched its range, and it's still doing so today. One of our problems now, however, is that the rate of population increase has—at least temporarily—outpaced our possible range expansion. In fact, it's very easy to calculate that in a few thousand years—at our present rate of procreation—the weight of human flesh and blood would be equal to that of the entire universe!

Plowboy: Then wouldn't you say that we're at a bottleneck right now? Isn't it true that there's no possible way to expand into space quickly enough to alleviate the problems of Earth's population growth?
Asimov: That's right. In the next half-century we can put, at most, tens of thousands of people into space. But if we continue to multiply as we're doing now, we'll add *billions* of individuals to the planet's population. So we have to solve *that* problem right here on Earth.

Plowboy: Do you have any ideas as to how we might best deal with overpopulation?
Asimov: There are only two methods: we can either increase the death rate or decrease the birth rate. Unless we use our ingenuity to lower the world's birth rate, we'll face the fate of every species that outgrows its food supply . . . and die off as a result of famine, disease, predation, and so on.
We *must*, therefore, lower the birth rate . . . and I think the best means of doing so is through universal *voluntary* contraception. To me, the logical way to achieve that goal is to give women something to do besides having a lot of children. Most societies have never *allowed* women to do anything important *other* than bear offspring. After all, during most of history, death rates were high . . . infant mortality rates were tremendous . . . and life

expectancy was low. So people had to produce a lot of children or the race would have died out.

Now, however, we've reversed the situation. The death rate is low, infant mortality is low, life expectancy is high, and we're going to destroy the Earth if we *continue* to reproduce at the present rate. So we should make it respectable for women *not* to have a lot of children.

Of course, my proposal is essentially the same as one of the key goals of the women's liberation movement. I've even been pronounced a radical feminist: not because I love women, although I do . . . and not because I think women's liberation is just and fair and decent, although I do . . . but because I believe we *have* to liberate women if the race is to survive.

Plowboy: But *finding* rewarding work for women would be easier in a prospering country like ours than in a poor land which isn't even able to keep many of its *present* work force employed.
Asimov: That *is* a problem. So what we have to do is go through a very difficult transition period in which we gradually distribute the food supply and goods of the world as evenly as possible. The prosperous nations will likely have to go through some hard times for the sake of the impoverished countries, an eventuality which will surely strike the people in the wealthy lands as unfair.

But then, every year when income tax comes due, I realize that I pay a lot of money to the government and get back very little in actual cash benefits . . . whereas poor people pay virtually *nothing* to the government and get unemployment compensation and all sorts of welfare services. So I think, "My God, they take from me and give to them. It's so unfair." But no, it's not unfair! Because, you see, I'm getting the advantages of a stable society as a result of the exchange!

And if the poorer people of the *world* don't start getting some benefits from the more prosperous ones, I'm afraid we're going to *lose* the limited global stability that we have. They aren't going to starve quietly . . . they're going to come and try to take our goods from us.

But the need to build up space—we've come back to space again—could motivate us to begin such necessary sharing.

Plowboy: It seems evident that we must cut back on our population growth. Do you also feel we need to cut back on our use of energy?

Asimov: A lot of people think that the United States should reduce its energy consumption. "We used only half as much energy in the early sixties as we do now," they say, "and life wasn't so bad then." There's only one catch to that argument: since the early sixties, the population of the Earth has gone up by over one billion, and much of our additional energy usage has allowed our nation—with 5 percent of the Earth's people—to export a great deal of food to the *rest* of the world. So anyone who wants us to cut our energy use in half should first make some of those one billion mouths disappear!

Now there are those who say that we can avoid the whole dilemma if we develop a more *labor*-intensive agriculture . . . that is, have more people—and fewer machines—working on our farms. Well, I want to hear folks who say we need more agricultural laborers volunteer to *become* such workers. The truth of the matter, though, is that most people who move from the cities to the country these days are not likely to become agricultural workers . . . they're suburban and exurban middle-class families who live in very comfortable houses.

And the individuals who say they *are* moving out to raise their own food and consume less of the world's resources are often the very ones who also, so to speak, bring their electric guitars with them . . . and want to be sure there's a nice modern hospital located in a convenient nearby city.

Such people don't realize that technology is not something you can break up into little fragments. It's all of a piece.

Plowboy: Don't you feel that men and women can make use of modern technology and still try to live more self-reliant, less energy-wasteful, and more environmentally sound lifestyles.

Asimov: Yes, certainly we can all eliminate waste. As far as I know, there isn't anyone in the *world* who advocates using more energy than is absolutely necessary.

Plowboy: In other words, you feel it's *overwhelmingly* important that we control population growth . . . and yet you almost *casually* take it for granted that we should reduce our wasteful energy and resource consumption. I could just as well counter your position by saying that nobody in his or her right mind could argue with limiting population, and—since it's been estimated that our country could cut its energy consumption almost in *half* simply by properly insulating buildings and establishing co-generation facilities in industrial plants—that we *urgently* need to address the issue of energy efficiency.

Asimov: Well, there's a difference between the two issues. There are, you see, no religious, moral, or social teachings that say using a lot of energy is a wonderful thing to do. Instead, when the price of energy goes up—or its availability goes down—almost *everyone* automatically makes a push for energy conservation. On the other hand, there *is* still much propaganda that advocates having children.

Plowboy: Would you also claim that it should be relatively easy to conserve our material resources . . . since there's no religion preaching "Thou shalt not recycle"?

Asimov: That's exactly right. Now I admit that we've moved in the wrong direction by cultivating planned obsolescence and conspicuous consumption. And it's going to be difficult to control waste as long as people see the ability to squander as a sign of status, and businesses feel that it's economically beneficial to make things that break down quickly.

Plowboy: How do we combat such practices?

Asimov: Well, you might argue that it's difficult to eliminate waste in a capitalist economy which is based on continually making unimportant product improvements in order to convince customers that one item is better than another. On the other hand, if we were to regulate such competition out of society, we *could* end up with the wastefulness of institutionalized inefficiency. So I'm not sure how best to deal with that problem.

Plowboy: Do you want to take a stab at suggesting a solution?

Asimov: I suppose we're going to have to indulge in peer group persuasion. How, for instance, can people be prevented from wearing eaglet feathers on their hats? The answer, of course is to put so much concern for conservation into the public mind that anyone who *does* wear an eaglet feather becomes *persona non grata* in respectable society. Perhaps the socially conscious minority can, in a similar manner, create a kind of spearhead movement for resource and energy conservation.

Plowboy: Dr. Asimov, your hope for the future is based on expansion into outer space. But do you feel that humankind could, instead, learn to be so truly efficient in, and conscious of, our use of energy and resources that we could stabilize our consumption—just as we need to stabilize our population—and survive perfectly well on Earth . . . *without* having to expand into space? A lot of thinkers believe that we can do so.

Asimov: I suppose you could argue that if we develop nuclear fusion—or *if* we somehow stabilize our population and energy demands—we might be able to survive indefinitely without leaving the surface of the Earth. But my own feeling is that even if we could manage it technologically and economically, human *psychology* would defeat the attempt. Earth would become a prison. There would be no unifying purpose to help us transcend the nation states . . . people would forever feel themselves to be ethnic groups, language groups, and racial groups . . . and we would be defeated eventually by our incessant quarreling.

I think that even if we *didn't* need space exploration to keep civilization alive for material reasons, we would need that expansion for—I almost hate to say the word—*spiritual* reasons!

Plowboy: So you consider expansion into nearby space to be essential.

Asimov: Yes. We've reached the stage where, if we don't *transcend* the Earth, we're going to destroy it. And I think that—over the next couple of centuries—it will be necessary for us to expand into the solar system generally. I don't see that goal as the *end*, either. Eventually we are going to make *all* of space our own!

Plowboy: How do you foresee the accomplishment of such a monumental goal?

Asimov: Well, the first steps have been easy . . . it took only three days to reach the moon. By comparison, Columbus had to travel—out of contact with "civilization"—for *weeks* to reach the New World.

But going to Mars, our next logical objective, will mean a round trip of months or even years. And that may be more of a *psychological* problem than it is a *technological* challenge. After all, we on Earth are used to a huge world and—if you view the planet as a spaceship—we're used to living on the *outside* of the hull. All our life support systems are on the surface and held in place by gravity.

The people who run any space settlements that we establish, however, will soon become accustomed to living in an *inside* world. Superficially, their environments may be very earthlike . . . because the settlements can be adjusted to have the appropriate gravitational effects, day and night lighting, and so on. Essentially, though, the space workers will be living "inside," be more aware of space, and be much more intimately concerned with the cycling of their resources—food, air, water, etc.—than we Earthlings are.

And the hundreds of thousands, or maybe even millions, of people manning such settlements will—over the years—become as used to space travel as we are to going about in a plane or an automobile. Such men and women will be psychologically comfortable in an exploratory spaceship . . . the vessel will be much more like the home they've lived in all their lives than *Earth* would be!

So I anticipate that our space settlers *will* be able to undertake long voyages which would be psychologically impossible for Earth dwellers. They *will* be able to establish settlements within asteroids. They'll be the footloose Vikings of the future. The rest of us will, indeed, be prisoners of Earth.

Plowboy: You envision settlements *inside* of asteroids?
Asimov: Yes, those pioneers could hollow out the mini-planets. The asteroids would—by the way—make for much *better* settlements than would the moon, because that satellite doesn't have certain lightweight elements . . . including carbon, hydrogen, and nitrogen. Lunar residents would therefore have to depend on the Earth for such basic substances, but settlers of the asteroids could have their own supplies and be truly *independent* of Earth.

Moreover, if such explorers developed nuclear fusion, they might even eventually become completely independent of the *sun* . . . and be able to pilot their asteroids into outer space.

Plowboy: Why send an asteroid off into space?
Asimov: Ah, because *then* the travelers could explore the stars without ever leaving home. They wouldn't have to abandon the world they've lived in . . . *or* have to say goodbye to their friends and relatives and all the old familiar places. Instead, the whole asteroid could just stop going around the

sun and take off. Eventually—after a long, long time—the explorers' descendants might reach another planetary system.

Plowboy: But the nearest solar system is light years away.

Asimov: Granted, a huge time factor is involved in all this, so it's difficult for you and me to see how people could possibly undertake such a trip. But I can imagine speaking to an amoeba—if you'll allow me to imagine an amoeba capable of discussing the matter—and asking how it would like to be one of fifty trillion cells making up a multicellular organism such as a man . . . a creation in which the *individual* amoeba didn't count at all. The tiny cell might be horrified at the suggestion. "What?!" it would say. "Give up my consciousness and individuality just to be part of a large group? Never, never, never!"

Yet as each of us—as the consciousness of our combined fifty trillion cells—knows, there are things we can do and pleasures we can experience that an individual cell can't even imagine. You or I can't help feeling that it's worthwhile for our cells to give up their independence and individuality for the sake of what we have.

Well, I feel a *reverse* development may someday occur on a grander scale. An individual asteroid settlement will decide not to be part of a large community of settlements, will prefer to go off by itself and become an "amoeba" again . . . for the sake of eventually establishing a *new* planetary "individual" under completely new circumstances.

Of course, it's hard to see into the future with accuracy. It may be—in fact, it's almost inevitable—that once we start moving out into space, events will take a completely unexpected turn. Some new development will occur which will afterward appear so obvious that future generations will wonder why *we* didn't foresee it.

Plowboy: Dr. Asimov, I'd like for us to come back to Earth now, so I can ask you about one more issue. What do you think of man's relationship with nature? Do you see it as, say, a human using a tool . . . observing something pretty . . . or interacting with a symbiotic equal?

Asimov: Well, you're personifying nature, while I see nature as *encompassing* man. We've had an ecological balance on Earth, and we don't want our race to upset that balance. But it may be that—as a result of man's movement in space—we will eventually create an altered ecology that is even more to our liking!

Space settlements won't be made entirely of metal and glass and concrete. There will be areas given over to agriculture, to the raising of plants and small animals . . . both those species that are useful and some others that aren't necessary but please us aesthetically. But we'll want to *exclude* disease germs, or plants and animals that we would consider harmful. So we'll try to form a kind of simplified ecology that includes only those "companions" that we find beneficial in some way.

Plowboy: I was really wondering what role you see for the natural world on *Earth*. Do you see that world as intrinsically important?
Asimov: It is important in that it's loaded with variety. Anything that's done to decrease that variety is likely to lessen the natural world's value and usefulness. On the other hand, ecological balances have shifted constantly through the history of life . . . and have sometimes done so drastically. We can't suppose that there is some cosmic rule which says the ecology must exist forever as it exists now.

And, in fact, I look forward to a multiplicity of human habitats *and* a multiplicity of *ecologies*! Not only will we have the enormous lifework and interdependence of Earth's natural system—one that I would be reluctant to see us interfere with—but we would have *other* habitats, each with its own ecological lacework. The sum total may represent a new level of complication beyond that which we have now.

Space settlers may someday feel sorry for Earth residents, who have only one limited ecology and are so much at the mercy of their natural environment.

Plowboy: Those are interesting points. Still, it seems as if every time I ask you about Earth's environment, you end up talking about space again.
Asimov: I guess for me everything *does* come back to space. Maybe that's because I've been writing science fiction all these years . . . but I definitely believe that humanity's destiny will be found in expansion beyond our planet's surface.

I told you before that I'm pessimistic about our short term future, and I am. But if we *do* manage to solve the immediate problems, to control population, to achieve some sort of international cooperation, and to move out into space . . . then after that, I'm very optimistic. It may be shortsighted-ness on my part that I fail to see the obstacles behind those that now exist, or that I dismiss those future predicaments by saying, "Well, we'll be able to solve them."

And maybe I'm wrong. But it seems to me that if we can solve our immediate problems—those that will come up in the next three decades or so—and get out into space . . . we'll have relatively clear sailing from there on!

Isaac Asimov

Darrell Schweitzer / 1981

From *Science Fiction Voices #5* (San Bernardino, Calif.: The Borgo Press, 1981). Copyright © 1981. Reprinted by permission of Darrell Schweitzer.

DS: What differences have you noticed between the way space travel was depicted in early science fiction and the way it actually happened?

IA: Well, in science fiction space travel was a one-man operation usually, with the bright inventor inventing the damn thing and getting into the ship and sailing off to Deneb III, perhaps with his sidekick, perhaps with a villain; and in real life we know what happened. It was a team endeavor, and they went through an immense number of stages before they headed for the moon.

DS: Did it occur to you when you were writing stories in the 1940s that space travel would involve professional astronauts rather than somebody working in his back yard?

IA: Obviously not, you see, because the first story I ever wrote about a trip to the moon was exactly like any other science-fiction story—the inventor doing it himself.

DS: Are you pleased in the way that science-fiction predictions about space travel have come out?

IA: Well, I'm pleased with the fact that science-fiction people had complete faith in interplanetary travel when none of the "intelligent" did. The "intelligent" people never know what's going on anyway.

DS: When you were writing these early stories, could you come up with any practical reason for space travel: was it a dream of the stars or a chance to get rich?

IA: Well, I think that the history of exploration on Earth is primarily that of curiosity as to what is beyond the hill. Naturally, there's always the hope you'll find new room to live in. But I don't think in general that exploration on Earth has been the result of people trying to get new frying pans or something. Unfortunately, with space travel now we're expecting the general public to pay for it, and you have to promise them something in return. You want to reach the stars. They want new coatings for their frying pans. So you promise them new coatings for their frying pans.

DS: Can you think of any economic reason to colonize another planet?
IA: A trillion ones. For one thing, we're going to learn a great deal more, and the more knowledge we have, the more comfortable we're going to be able to make our lives. Secondly, by reaching out into space we may eventually learn how to tap solar energy out there and beam it down to Earth, so as to solve our energy crisis. Thirdly, we will have people living on a multiplicity of worlds so that if anything happens to any one of them, even to Earth, mankind will continue. Again, because people are living on other planets, and in colonies in space, these people will probably be better equipped to explore space than Earthmen are. The burden will fall upon them for the expansion of the human race.

DS: Carl Sagan is now saying that it's possible to terraform Venus by seeding algae into the upper atmosphere.
IA: It's conceivable. I don't think it's possible, but it's conceivable.

DS: How could we go about convincing anyone that this might be worthwhile, since it might not pay off for a hundred years?
IA: I don't know. Perhaps it will not be possible to persuade Congress. Perhaps the Soviet Union will do it. It doesn't matter to me who does it.

DS: Since experience has shown us that often things predicted by science fiction don't actually happen that way, will we ever have a problem in the field with writers not believing their own speculation?
IA: No. No one expects us to believe our science-fiction speculations. Science-fiction speculation isn't intended to be believed. It isn't intended to predict. It is merely a story. The only thing that science fiction predicts is that the future is going to be different from the present, and *that* will always come true. The future will be different from the present. And except for that, science fiction consists of cautionary tales. They tell you what might come true,

and if you like it you fight for it. If you don't like it, you fight against it. That's all. They don't tell you what will be true. Nobody knows.

DS: Then when you write a story, is it a case of "just suppose," or do you worry about the scientific feasibility of it?
IA: I worry about the scientific details, but I don't ask myself even for one moment whether this will really come to pass. In other words, if I have somebody reaching the star Deneb, I don't ask myself whether somebody will reach the star Deneb; but as long as they're there I try to describe Deneb as it really is. I don't call it a red dwarf.

DS: Do you ever worry about your own fiction dating?
IA: No, as a matter of fact I don't. Some of my stories date in the sense that they take place in a year which is now in the past. My story "Trends" takes place in 1973 and is all wrong. But even that doesn't date it because there is more to the story than just the events which take place in 1973. It's still an interesting story. And then a lot of my stories aren't going to date in my lifetime because I set them in the far future, and I involve myself with events which aren't likely to either come to pass or to clearly not come to pass. For instance, I can live a considerable time before I can worry about whether we're going to have robots as intelligent as human beings, or galactic empires, or if we're going to have time travel, or even an electronic pump. It's a mistake, I think, to write stories which try to catch tomorrow's headlines, because you may make good sales for now, but they will be dead next year.

DS: It seems that on that basis "Trends" should be dead, but people still read it. Why?
IA: That's because the story wasn't really written realistically. I mean, you take as an example Michael Crichton's *The Andromeda Strain*. What's the good now of reading excitedly about a virus brought back by astronauts when you know it's not going to happen? Or *On The Beach*, for instance? You know nuclear warfare is not going to work that way, so there's sort of a Victorian flavor to it. This is what I would like to avoid anyway. Of course, those stories may hit the best-seller lists, and maybe that's all the authors go for. Bless them. I go for other things.

DS: What do *you* go for?

IA: I would like to see to it that my books are read after I'm dead.

DS: What makes a science-fiction work last?

IA: I suppose what makes a science-fiction work last is that, as in all literature, it will have something to say to generations yet unborn. In other words, Shakespeare's plays don't have meaning only for the English people of 1600. They deal with human beings in such a way they have meaning for us today. While I don't pretend to be anywhere near Shakespeare, I would just like to get a little bit of that. For instance, the young people who read *The Foundation Trilogy* now, and who like it, and are pleased with it, are sometimes not aware that it was written thirty years before they were born. And yet, I don't think if one were to read *The Foundation Trilogy* that there'd be much of a sense of dating about it. You can't read it and tell yourself this is typical 1940s, because it isn't. At least not in my opinion.

DS: Untypical 1940s . . . One thing that strikes me as odd about the series is that it is based on the premise that history actually repeats itself in detail. Is it likely that there will be imperialism along Roman lines in outer space, as opposed to something entirely new?

IA: Probably not. There'll probably be something entirely new, and if I were writing it now I would try to make it something entirely new; and I might not succeed. This was written when I was in my twenties, and the only way I could do it was to repeat the Roman Empire, and I did it with the vigor and ignorance of the twenties—the age, not the decade. So there is something in it that appeals to people. I could do it much better now and probably fail. For instance, I wrote "Nightfall" when I was twenty-one. It's poorly written, but if I wrote it now I could write it much better, and it would be a much worse story. I needed that twenty-one-year-old-not-knowing-what-you're-doing sense in order to get it across.

DS: Then you've never been tempted to go back and tamper with your earlier work?

IA: No, no. Let it stand as it is, especially if it's been well received. You know, you don't want to break up a winning team.

DS: If you were to write a series now about the next thousand years of human history, how would you go about it without using the Roman model?

IA: Darned if I know. I've never given it any thought whatsoever. I obviously am never going to do it, because I'm never going to compete with *Foundation*. So, I have never thought about it.

DS: Well, in what direction would you like to go in science fiction right now?

IA: I may not go in any. I have written a straight murder mystery, and instead of taking seven months as a science-fiction novel takes me, it took me seven weeks, and I enjoyed it tremendously; and if it does well I may want to write some more murder mystery novels. I've written in the last four or five years twenty-six mystery short stories, and I enjoy them too. So I have this horrible feeling that after I've been a science-fiction writer for so many decades I want to be a mystery writer for a while.

DS: How about more science-fiction mysteries?

IA: Well anything that is science fiction is so damn hard to write. Science fiction is the hardest thing in the world to write, and I can say that better than anyone else can because I'm the only person I know who has written just about in all subjects, fiction and nonfiction, at all age levels, so I can compare different things; and to me it's clear that science fiction is the hardest thing to write, and it's not because I do it poorly. I do it very well. So that, my feeling is, if I can get away without doing science fiction as I grow older and lazier, I would like to. Nevertheless, I am writing science fiction at the present moment, with several stories in press. I've got a science-fiction story written that I haven't succeeded in selling yet, believe it or not. I've tried it in three places, but none of them are science-fiction magazines. It was originally written for *Seventeen,* and I hesitate to show it to science-fiction magazines because they may be tempted to take it on my name only, and since I wrote it for teenagers, the readers in the science-fiction magazines might not like it. So I'm waiting to see if there's a logical outlet for it. I'm not hurting for money, so I can afford to let a story sit around.

DS: Since you're not hurting for money, do you ever still want to write science fiction for the love of it?

IA: It's the only reason I write it, because there's nothing I write that pays me so small a sum per hour as science fiction. My *F&SF* essays pay me a little less

than three cents a word, which is the least I get for anything I write, but my
F&SF essays take me a day apiece, and they're fun, so I'm willing. A science-
fiction story the same length would take me a week, and it wouldn't get me
much more. So anytime I write science fiction it's for the fun of it, unless
maybe I were to write another Foundation novel, because Doubleday is anxious enough for it to be willing to bribe me heavily, and the paperbacks
would probably bribe me heavily. But writing another Foundation novel is a
frightening thing to me, because I have a feeling that I would write it much
more skillfully and it would be much poorer, and that all the science-fiction
fans would say, "Read the first three books. Don't read that fourth one. It's no
good." I hate to do that. [See update at end of interview.]

DS: If science fiction is the most difficult type of writing, why did you start
there, when presumably at the age of twenty-one or so you didn't know as
much about writing as you do now?
IA: Because that's all I wanted to write. I wasn't writing to make a living
when I started. I was writing because I wanted to write, and this was what I
wanted to write. It was only much later on that I discovered I could write
other things too, easier things that made more money. And I still write science fiction because the love lingers.

DS: What are your writing methods like?
IA: Absolutely nothing to describe. I sit down at the typewriter and type.

DS: One draft?
IA: No, no. I write it up, go over it and make corrections in pen and ink, and
then I type it up a second time. Everything goes through the typewriter twice.

DS: Do you write from the top of your head, say an article you read in a magazine which has an idea you can make a good story out of, or do you work
more from the subconscious?
IA: Oh no, I think. I don't let inspiration strike. What I usually do is I get
some basic notion. Then I think up a problem involving it. Then I think up a
resolution. After I have a problem and the resolution, I think up a place to
begin. And then I start, and I write toward the resolution. The details I make
up as I go along. I never outline. Even my most complicated novels were
never outlined.

DS: Do you worry about *how* it's going to be written, or let that take care of itself?

IA: No. I never worry about it. When I first started off I figured if I couldn't finish a story I'd throw it away. I think maybe once or twice I couldn't. But once I'd been writing for about two years I finished every story I started. It's just too late to worry about it now.

DS: A few years back, when we had something called "The New Wave," and everybody was letting off verbal fireworks, did you have any inclination to join in?

IA: None—because I can't. The sort of stuff that Harlan Ellison writes, that Barry Malzberg writes, or John Brunner wrote with *Stand On Zanzibar*, is something I can't do. And I don't believe in trying to do something I can't do. I write what I write. If the time comes when people don't want it, then I won't be able to sell. If people continue to want it, then I will sell. There's no urgency to try to keep up with the fashions. I just do what I can.

DS: When you started writing did you try to write what was then fashionable?

IA: Well, what happened was I started writing, and I liked Weinbaum and Nat Schachner—I tried to write like that. And as time went on I liked Clifford Simak and enjoyed Robert Heinlein, and my writing automatically bent in that direction. Now my writing may bend in the direction of Harlan Ellison, because everytime I read a story of his I admire and envy it and wish I could have written it; but it can't bend very far, because the talent isn't there. Still, my mystery, *Murder at the ABA*, is definitely not in my usual style. There is more sex in it, more realism, although not very much. If Harlan were writing it there'd be a lot more.

DS: Is this really a difference in talent, or just personality, a case of a writer writing one sort of story because that's who he is?

IA: There are some writers who have many styles, I'm sure, who can imitate different fashions. I can't. My talents are very limited. In fiction I tell very straightforward stories, with very unadorned style; and in nonfiction my great talent is to explain difficult things simply without becoming inaccurate. And these are not very important talents, but they're enough, so I can make a living.

DS: What writers outside the science-fiction field have had any influence on you?

IA: As far as my writing is concerned? None. I admire writers like Shakespeare. It sounds phoney to say I admire Shakespeare, but I wrote a two-volume book on him, so I think I can claim to admire him, and I am very fond of Dickens, and I am very fond of Wodehouse, but I've never tried to imitate them, either consciously or unconsciously. Agatha Christie, whom I have also admired, has had a great influence on my murder mysteries, and maybe even on my science-fiction mysteries. There's also G. K. Chesterton. But except for them, all the rest are science-fiction people. And even with Christie and Chesterton—they're category fiction writers too. I mean, none of the first great Literary Lights influenced me, because either I didn't read them, or I read them without being able to be influenced by them.

DS: How do you feel about the science-fiction label? Lately there have been a lot of people saying we should remove it. Do you think this will do any good?

IA: Well, let me tell you a story. Once, people objected to the smell of Camembert cheese, so they took off all the labels saying "Camembert cheese," and they wrote on them "rose petals." Do you think the smell changed? Okay. Science fiction is science fiction. Call it anything else you want and it's still science fiction. If people don't want to write science fiction then they don't write science fiction. If they want to call it speculative fiction, they can call it speculative fiction, but if they write rotten science fiction, calling it speculative fiction won't make it good speculative fiction. If they write good science fiction, but think the phrase is a drag and hurts sales, and they want to call it speculative fiction, they have a right to, and I hope they sell better. But as for me, I'm sticking to science fiction, because when I write science fiction that's what I write. The important thing is to write good stuff, I think, whatever they call it.

DS: What do you think would happen if a science-fiction novel of yours was released as general fiction?

IA: I think my fans would buy it in the same numbers that they would buy it if it were called science fiction, and that the people who never heard of me would continue not to buy it. I don't think it would make any difference in sales whatsoever.

DS: Do you think there are people who would not buy your books because they're labelled science fiction?

IA: Well, if people buy my stuff because they don't realize it's science fiction, they won't like it anyway because it will be science fiction. All my nonfiction stuff—much of it anyway—is sometimes put in the science-fiction category. In other words, you'll go through the science-fiction shelves and you'll see *An Easy Introduction to the Slide Rule* by Isaac Asimov. In fact, I once got a phone call from someone who said, "Do you realize that at a certain bookstore they've got *An Easy Introduction to the Slide Rule* in with the science fiction?" I said, "I don't care. My science-fiction readers buy my nonfiction too. In other words, in my particular case—I don't say this is true for other writers—all my books fall into a particular category, "Asimov fiction," and there are people who will buy anything that I write, and there are people who will buy nothing that I write. And any category that I place it under other than Asimov isn't going to change it.

DS: Haven't you wanted to proselytize for science fiction by reaching new readers?

IA: As a matter of fact, I do that all the time. I'm constantly writing articles on science fiction in non-science fiction journals. I've written articles in places like the *Humanist, Intellectual Digest, Smithsonian Magazine*. I've written an article on science fiction in the *Britannica Yearbook of Science and the Future*, for instance. I've made speeches about science fiction in all sorts of places, including the American Association for the Advancement of Science. So I'm a very active proselytizer at all times.

DS: If you were to publish a science-fiction story in, say, *Playboy*, would it be recognized as science fiction? A lot of people seem to feel if they don't call something science fiction they have a better chance of selling it to a bigger magazine.

IA: Well, I don't know. They might say so, but how can you tell? I had a science-fiction story in the *New York Times Magazine* section, for instance, on January 5, 1975. I don't know if it was labelled science fiction. It was called "The Life and Times of Multivac" and you couldn't read two paragraphs without knowing it was science fiction. If you're just against reading science fiction on principle, you're not going to read that story. I don't know how many people read it and how many didn't.

DS: In your early days did you find that you tended to get categorized as a "pulp writer"?

IA: That's what I was. I *was* a pulp writer, just as I'm now a science-fiction writer. I'm not ashamed of where I started. That's where I wanted to start. And there's nothing wrong with being a pulp writer. I wanted to be a pulp writer, so I became a pulp writer. I wanted to be a science-fiction writer, so I became a science-fiction writer, and to this day I'm not ashamed of it.

DS: You make a difference between the two.

IA: A science-fiction writer was one of the categories of pulp writer in those days. A pulp writer was someone who wrote for the pulp magazines, and in order to make a living, or to make any serious amount of money writing for the pulp magazines, you had to write a lot. And I learned how to write fast and in great quantity. I've now published over two hundred books. I've learned my lesson. If that doesn't make me a pulp writer, what does?

DS: Can you still be a pulp writer when you're writing books?

IA: Well, as now there are scarcely any pulp magazines, you can't be a pulp writer literally. I'm a pulp writer in the sense that I still write fast, as well as a wide variety of things. That was another thing a pulp writer had to do if he wanted to make a living. He had to write all kinds of things, because you couldn't make a living from just one magazine. So I learned how to write fast and a whole lot of different things.

DS: Do you write your best work fast?

IA: I would like to be able to answer that, but I write everything at the same speed—top.

DS: Has it always been that way?

IA: Always.

DS: You mentioned that it takes you seven months to write some novels.

IA: Right, it takes me seven months to write some novels, one month for others, not because I spend more time at the typewriter, but because I spend more time in between doing other things. In other words, when I write my murder mysteries, things go sufficiently easily that I can sit there day after day and work at it. When I write a science-fiction story, the thinking up of things, working out the society, and so on, is such that I maybe don't work oftener than one evening a week on it. The rest of the time is thinking time; I'm doing other typing. If you could take all the typing I actually did in the seven months and squish it together, it would come out seven weeks just like the other one.

DS: But basically there's more mental work to it.
IA: Yes.

[Update: since giving this interview, Asimov has contracted with Doubleday for a fourth Foundation novel, *Lightning Rod.*]

Science and American Society

Fred Jerome / 1981

Mr. Asimov is a biochemist and science writer of more than *two hundred* books. The interviewer is Fred Jerome, Information Director of the Scientists' Institute for Public Information in New York.

FJ: Dr. Asimov, you have written several works offering a scientific guide to various parts of the Bible. Your latest book, *In the Beginning*, provides an in-depth analysis of the first eleven chapters of *Genesis*. In view of this, how do you feel about the increasing influence of what is called "creationism" and the political influence of the new wave of religious fundamentalists?

IA: I think it is most pernicious, and something to be fought in every way possible. I believe that the so-called "moral majority" is attempting to put blinders over the American mind, to remold public opinion in its own fashion, and to put an end to any scientific advance in the United States that isn't directly related to weapons and warfare. And I fear that, if the moral majority were to gain its ends, a dark age would descend upon the United States.

FJ: As this country's leading popularizer of science and science fiction, how do you feel about the recent report from the U.S. Department of Education which says that most Americans are headed towards "virtual scientific and technological illiteracy"?

IA: First, I'm not sure I ought to allow myself to be called the foremost science popularizer, because these days, I think by general consent the person holding that post is Carl Sagan. As to my feeling about the statement on illiteracy, I totally agree, except that I don't think this is something new. The American population, indeed the population of any nation, has always been largely scientifically illiterate; the danger is not so much that not enough people are going to know about science but rather that in some camps, science is viewed as the enemy. It's one thing not to understand science, and it's another completely to misunderstand science—to have people feel that scientists and technologists are evil, that their intentions are dangerous, and that only in healthful ignorance can we find salvation.

FJ: Would you say that this attitude toward scientists is a recent development?
IA: There has always been a certain amount of anti-intellectualism in the United States, but now it is focusing in upon science. There are many persons in this country with a considerable amount of education who know nothing about science, who feel that, because they've learned the terminology, they can lead the fight against science, and do so effectively.

FJ: To what do you attribute this anti-science trend?
IA: For one thing, a major problem with science—something which is at the same time its greatest value to those of us who are science-minded—is its uncertainty, its incompleteness, its openness; that new discoveries are made and that the old ones are invariably tentative; that there is controversy over certain facts. All this gives people the feeling that scientists don't really know what they're talking about. Instead, they would rather turn to non-scientists—people who espouse thoughts which are complete, final, absolutely certain, and who, like the Bible, "have all the answers." People want certainty. They don't want to be told that two and two may very well be four—until further evidence comes in. They would prefer to be told that two and two is definitely five and a half.

Another problem with science is that people confuse *knowledge* with the *uses* to which knowledge is put. In other words, if politicians, if economists, if industrialists all misuse scientific knowledge for their own short-term gains and, in the process, produce damage of one sort or another, the blame turns upon the scientists who have uncovered the knowledge and who, paradoxically, may be the only ones fighting against such misuse. For example, while it was scientists who made the nuclear bomb possible, it was also they who, from the very start, objected to its use.

FJ: You wrote in *Saturday Review* that "the decline in American world power is in part, at least, brought about by our diminishing status as a world science leader. If our problems are to be solved, it will be through the medium of science and technology." Where does American technology stand today, and is it competitive with that of other nations?

IA: I think that the American technological structure is decaying, that our industries are not in the forefront of technological development. I believe that respect for science is declining, as well as the numbers of young people we are training in science, and that even those whom we are training, we are training poorly. Thus the effect will be a continuing one. The most spectacular aspect of American technology in the last decade—space exploration—is being dismantled. Other nations, notably Japan, are taking over our leadership role in technology, and the Soviet Union is gaining on us in various aspects of technology. Even Western Europe is advancing technologically, which suggests that, if the situation isn't changed, the United States will become a decaying power.

FJ: Do you see any developments in this country which show a promise of reversing this decline?

IA: I see an increasing amount of grassroots support for the U.S. space effort and a growing realization that our going out into space is absolutely essential, not only for our own economy but for the world economy; that in order to be able to support our population, to be able to replace the decaying resource content of the Earth's crust, we are dependent on the resources of space.

FJ: Do you anticipate any changes in science policy under the Reagan administration? Do you think the administration's emphasis to date on applied technology and defense spending will hurt or help our country's scientific enterprise, and thus our world leadership position?

IA: In view of his support of the creationist viewpoint and his campaign criticism of evolution, my feeling is that President Reagan is not particularly science-minded. Therefore, I think that, given his general intention to cut government spending, he will cut any appropriations devoted to extending our scientific and technological knowledge unless he can be convinced that it has a direct and immediate application to defense technology. I imagine that a great many scientists will now, out of self-defense, have to justify their projects on the basis that whatever it is they're doing will help us militarily. You know what they'll say: the paperclips we make will hold together the plans which will be used to build a new bomb, and so forth. And no doubt this will work to a certain extent. All in all, I believe we are in for a dry spell under Reagan, and this is sad.

FJ: Do you think there is a chance that the space program, which not only enjoys popular support but also has a definite military component, might be an exception to that "dry spell"?

IA: I suspect that the administration will want more "spy" and other defense-oriented satellites, but they are not going to be pushing, for instance, for solar power satellites because Reagan seems to believe thoroughly that all we have to do to find more oil is to look for it.

FJ: Any possibility that the Reagan administration is likely to appoint a science adviser, or a science advisory committee, who might have some effect on these policies? I mean, Eisenhower had Kistiakowsky, and there were other science advisers for other presidents who urged some forward-looking policies . . .

IA: I believe that Nixon, however, lost interest in such things, and I'm afraid that Reagan has lacked interest in them from the start. Those who most eagerly support Reagan, are, I feel, suspicious of scientists, whom they suspect of being liberals.

FJ: If you were appointed science adviser, which policies would you make top priority?

IA: The computerization of technology, together with the exploration and exploitation of space. And while I would want to see robots pushed, at the same time I would want to see certain social changes advanced to prevent a developing robot and space technology from having too negative an effect on human beings as far as displacement and job loss are concerned.

You can't have technological advance and social change without trying to take into account its effect on human beings. I think of what happened during the first Industrial Revolution in Great Britain and the absolute horror of the factory system in those early decades of the nineteenth century, before the reformers succeeded in gaining acceptance for their humane principles and demonstrated that more humane treatment of workers can lead to increased profits. Today, we must ensure that certain measures are taken to prevent the present technological revolution from again producing human misery on a grand scale and we have to avoid callously fluffing off such a situation by saying, "Well, that's the way it is if we're going to advance."

FJ: Could you be more specific about the social measures you would advocate in order to avoid these dehumanizing effects?

IA: First, we have to educate people for membership in computerized society—to see to it that they understand computers, know how to use them, and aren't made obsolete by them. At the same time, we have to ensure that those people who are either too old or too tempermentally unsuited to work with computerized equipment will be able to locate jobs where knowledge of computerization isn't essential. This is a task for economists or social scientists, who, I assume, would know specifically how this should be done.

FJ: Recently there have been a number of cover-story articles in prominent science magazines dealing with society's fear of computers. According to all these articles, there is a fear that there's going to be an elite core of trained technicians running the vitals of society—which will all be computerized—and that this group will have a tremendous amount of power simply by virtue of their knowledge of this technology. Is "computer literacy" among our young people a way of dealing with this problem and, if so, what steps are the educational community, social planners, or the government taking to help them acquire such literacy?

IA: That I don't know. But I do know that people who are worrying about this are already too late. Throughout our lives we are at the mercy of many different groups of "experts" who run things we don't know how to operate, that we can't guide in any way. For example, if there's a school custodians' strike, the schools have to close; a rail strike, the cities could starve. In each instance, we can only depend upon the experts' good will and expertise. The computer issue is just one more situation in which we find ourselves at the mercy of a group of experts.

FJ: What is the possibility of—and the danger in—our creating an army of robot-experts whom we will be even less able to guide and control?

IA: When you're a passenger in an airplane, how sure are you that the pilot is a good one, that he happens not to be drunk at the time, or ill? At every step during the day, you are placing your life in the hands of people whose expertise you can't judge. If we indeed think that computer experts are just going to be button-pushers, then I should think more and more people would want to learn about computers—so they can check on this, so they can work things for themselves.

FJ: Is this aversion of yours to flying a reflection of your estimate of modern technology?

IA: Oh, no. I am sure, despite my previous remark, that the pilots of airplanes by and large are capable and educated, and are perfectly safe. You understand I was merely using it as an example. The reason that I don't fly is a purely irrational fear. It is by no means a carefully thought-out estimate of the dangers involved because I drive freely and without concern on the highways on holiday weekends, and that is a much more dangerous thing to do than taking an airplane, and I *know* it. This is purely irrational. Everyone has his irrational fears—this happens to be mine.

FJ: To come back to "robotics," isn't this a term you developed yourself?
IA: I invented the word, yes, without knowing it. I thought it was an everyday word.

FJ: It seems as if many people today are talking and writing about the possibility of "artificial intelligence," as it is called. Do you envision, in the near future, computers which will be capable of complicated thought, and even expressions of emotion; and do you think scientists should pursue such a goal?
IA: Robots are advancing with great rapidity, far more rapidly than I anticipated. When I started writing my robot stories forty years ago, I did not really expect to see robots in my lifetime. Of course, the robots we see today are nowhere nearly as intelligent as those in my stories, but we are advancing. However, I am not concerned about their becoming "intelligent."

We must not look upon intelligence as a kind of unitary thing, that is, we must not assume that if two widely different objects are both intelligent, they must necessarily be of equivalent or identical intelligence. For example, we suspect there may be such a thing as dolphin intelligence, but, even granting that, it is sufficiently different from our own human intelligence to preclude cross-species communication.

Unlike human intelligence, which has developed over three billion years out of proteins and nucleic acids by random changes, through the pressure of natural selection and with the single goal of *survival*, robots and computers are manufactured out of metal and electricity and solid state switches, a process which has only been going on for forty years at the most. Moreover, it has not been random change, but change by human guidance, and its ultimate goal is not survival but *the uses imposed upon them* by human beings. In view of these underlying differences, we might suspect that these two intelligences—even if equal quantitatively—might be very different qualitatively.

In fact, we can already see that it is so: computers in some respects, such as in their ability to perform arithmetical operations incredibly more rapidly and accurately than human beings, are already far ahead of us. And it may be that this is what computers and robots are best suited for—performing repetitive tasks and doing them rapidly whereas human beings specialize in seeing things as a whole, making judgments intuitively, insightfully, creatively. Now, it's difficult to see how computers can be programmed to perform these latter functions since we don't fully understand how *we* are able to do them. And even if we could program computers in this way, we would probably choose not to do so—not necessarily out of fear, but rather because it makes sense to specialize and to establish a symbiotic relationship in which both humans and robots together can advance further than either could separately.

There's not any danger of the computer replacing us. They will supplement us, and, for that matter, we will supplement them.

FJ: I'm wondering whether there might not be a contradiction between that optimistic view of the future of man and technology and your previously voiced concern about the power of those specialists who, both as individuals and as a group, are capable of acting on self-serving motives.

IA: The answer to that is that there is no *one* future; human beings make the future out of a vast array of possibilities. I prefer to consider the future in terms of the *ideal*, wherein all people act sanely and with judgment and decency.

Who is to say that we will? Well, if we do not, we can end up within a generation with a radioactive Earth. We can destroy ourselves in nuclear war, we can refuse to look at the difficulties of increasing population, and we can starve ourselves to death. We can, should we constantly look at only the short-term goals of our particular segment of the human race, kill ourselves in local wars and border skirmishes; or we can, should we perpetuate social injustice and inequities, destroy ourselves by our own violence and crime.

All of these possibilities exist, but so does the potentiality of behaving decently and, in so doing, creating for ourselves a perfectly marvelous future. A Russian journalist to whom I expressed this belief during a recent interview called me a "political vegetarian"—meaning, I think, that I was too caught up in goodness and niceness in a world in which such commodities do not, in reality, exist, and that I was unwilling to discuss instead the way we can convert the real world into a smoothly functioning, advanced machine. My response to that would be that I don't believe we can turn the world, as it now exists, into such a machine, but neither am I content to believe that the world cannot be otherwise than it is. It may not choose to be otherwise, but it could be.

FJ: Which of these trends do you feel is gaining the upper hand today?
IA: My view changes according to what I see in the morning paper. Whenever I read of some atrocity committed because of something that scarcely seems worthwhile, something which has occurred because someone's so-called "national honor" is at stake, then my spirits fall and I begin to think we won't make it. However, when I reflect on the recent hostage crisis and see the out-pouring of good will the human species is capable of and consider that during the 444 days of tension and crisis, those with their fingers on the bombs did not lose their tempers, nor behave stupidly, then I feel a little better about the world's chances.

FJ: To return to our previous discussion about the uncertainty of science, do you see a tendency among the popular science media—the magazines and TV series—to emphasize phenomena, breakthroughs, discoveries and to ignore the uncertainties, the mysteries, the questions?
IA: That depends. The stories run the gamut. Obviously, in order to maintain circulation, magazines must present something that will attract readers, and all too often that material is concerned with the fringe areas of science or the breakthroughs—and the wonder of it all. At the same time, there are publications that are more responsible and that don't try to buy readers at the cost of scientific ethics.

FJ: David Suzuki, who is a professor of zoology at the University of British Columbia and popular TV-show host in Canada, recently expressed sharp disappointment with television as a medium for educating the public in science and cited its failure to get across the most important lesson of science: "critical thinking." Do you agree?
IA: We could hardly expect a TV show to be popular if it consisted only, say, of Isaac Asimov being philosophical and discussing the problem of critical thinking. What the visual media needs is something splashy, special effects which give the viewer something to look at. That takes time and money, and doesn't leave much room for careful discussion . . . which, as I just said, could be expected to drive away viewers anyway.

FJ: A generation ago, after the first Soviet sputnik was successfully launched, American schools got a tremendous infusion of science and technology programs. Given that boost, how do you explain the "virtual scientific and technological illiteracy" which you, and the U.S. Department of Education, believe to be descriptive of the state of so many in the nation today?

IA: We can give the schools all kinds of money and all kinds of equipment for teaching science. But what we continually fail to give them is teachers who know science. Nor can we expect to solve the problem overnight, by throwing money at it. Rather, it's a slow process, one which requires gradual change. We have to teach the teachers first. And we have to stick with it.

The trouble is that all of this worked as long as we thought the Russians were ahead; but once we reached the moon, we said, "That's it," and we quit. Yes, we would have been a lot better off today if the Russians had stayed ahead of us.

FJ: As a former science teacher yourself, have you any specific approaches or improvements which you would recommend be introduced in science education?

IA: I really don't know. Every once in a while I feel drawn to what Garfield once said: that a real education was Mark Hopkins on one end of the log and a student at the other end. We are still at the point where good teachers are crucial to the education of students. While I hope that computerization will soon make it possible for students to make truly effective use of educational machines—to gather knowledge from a computerized library, and to study on one's own time and in one's own way—students will always need someone to turn to for advice and for an overall view of the material, that is, good teachers. Unfortunately, how we're going to get and keep them, in view of the low salaries and low respect they've traditionally commanded in this country, is still the problem today.

FJ: In 1979 you wrote that "since my hundredth book, my science-fiction production has decreased a great deal." What caused this shift in emphasis in your writing and what are you working on now?

IA: I can't quite explain how I go from one thing to another; these enthusiasms just seize me. The big change for me came at the time the first sputnik went up, when I became aware of the fact that the United States needed to be more scientifically minded and that I could write good science books. I suddenly felt that what I should be doing was to use my expertise for that end.

What I failed to anticipate was that publishers were also eager for science books at the time, so that I found myself scribbling them out as fast as I could write and making a reputation for myself as a science writer. Unable to say "no" to these projects, I left myself no time for fiction writing and no time to think about it. Now, however, my publishers are clamoring for a novel, even though I am currently at work on four huge nonfiction projects. They say: "We don't care." Of course they don't care. *I'm* the one who has to face those blank sheets of paper.

A Conversation with Isaac Asimov

Frank Kendig / 1982

From *Psychology Today*, vol. 17 (January 1983): 42–47. Copyright © 1983 Sussex Publishers, Inc. Reprinted with permission from Psychology Today Magazine.

I first met Isaac Asimov sometime in 1971. I don't remember the exact date, but I suspect that he does. Asimov seems to remember everything. I met him because of business: he was a writer, I was an editor, and we went through the usual negotiations. I do remember that he delivered the story early, some weeks before the deadline. Since then, I have bought a number of stories from him, for one magazine or another, and always the stories were delivered early. That's the way he is.

I can tell you some other things about him. He answers his own phone, and until recently was listed in the telephone book. He does not have a secretary. He was born in Russia in a town called Petrovichi on January 2, 1920. He weighed five pounds. He came to the United States when he was three years old and was brought up in Brooklyn. He began to write in 1931, when he was eleven, and got his first typewriter when he was fifteen—a second-hand Underwood upright that cost his father $10. His first publication was an essay in a school magazine published in 1934 when he was fourteen. He received his Ph.D. in biochemistry in 1948 from Columbia University. He published his first book in 1950, a novel called *Pebble in the Sky*.

His output since then is well known. He has published more than two hundred and sixty books at last count, which is a feat more distinguished by the variety and quality of the books than sheer numbers. Other writers have surpassed his output, but none have addressed as many subjects. Besides his forty or so science-fiction novels and mysteries, he has written perhaps one hundred and fifty books on various aspects of science. His books on difficult scientific subjects are so straightforward and clear that he is sometimes called the great explainer. I learned much of what I know about science from Isaac

Asimov, and I suspect that many of you, from scientist to schoolteacher, can honestly make the same statement. And he does not only write about science. Among his collected works are a two-volume guide to Shakespeare, an annotated *Paradise Lost*, an annotated *Don Juan*, and even five volumes of *Lecherous Limericks*.

Despite his prodigious output, Isaac Asimov now has a book on the best-seller lists for the first time. The book is *Foundation's Edge*, and it is the long-awaited sequel to his *Foundation* trilogy, first published in the early 1950s. At the core of all four *Foundation* novels is the concept of psychohistory—the prediction of human behavior by mathematical equations. It is a fictional concept, but one that may deserve serious attention.

I visited Asimov in his apartment overlooking New York City's Central Park to conduct the following interview. But before we go on, there is one more thing I can tell you about Isaac Asimov:

He is a nice man, a very nice man indeed.

—Frank Kendig

Kendig: How did you come up with the idea for the *Foundation* series?
Asimov: Well, let me see. I began the series in 1942, when I was a graduate student in chemistry and well acquainted with the kinetic theory of gases. The idea for what I call psychohistory came from the kinetic theory, which says that if you have a sizable sample of gas—quintillions of quintillions of atoms or molecules—you can predict exactly how the sample will act. The motion of any one atom or molecule is completely unpredictable—you can't tell where, in which direction, or how fast it will move—but you can average all the motions and from this deduce the gas laws.

It occurred to me that this might also be true for human beings. A human by himself is quite unpredictable, but a mob is usually a little more predictable. What if we applied a kinetic theory of humans to some future time, when there were millions of planets full of people? It seemed to me that it might be possible to work out mathematically what their reaction to a given stimulus might be.

Kendig: Possible in fact, or just in fiction? Did you think—do you think—that psychohistory would actually work?
Asimov: Well, at the time I was simply a young chemist trying to simplify a problem and draw a fictional analogy. The fact of the matter is that you cannot equate a human being with a gas molecule.

Even in a relatively small quantity of gas—eighteen grams of water vapor, for instance—there are something on the order of 10^{23} molecules, whereas in the galaxy as I imagined it, with millions of inhabited worlds, there would be only about 10^{15} human beings. That means only one hundred-millionth as many human beings in my future galaxy as there are molecules in eighteen grams of water vapor. And each human being is unimaginably more complicated than a molecule, so you can't really expect that psycho-history is going to be anywhere near as accurate as the kinetic theory of gases.

This is a problem for futurists. We have books by such writers as Spengler and Toynbee where they track how entire societies are born, develop, grow sick, and then die—using one society as a sort of norm and forcing all others into it. It has never seemed to me that these approaches could be reasonably predictive. Speaking as a professional futurist, I don't think that anyone can really predict anything but sort of vast gray sweeps.

Kendig: The people of the *Second Foundation* are portrayed as what I would call the ultimate psychologists. But there was a gap of more than thirty years between the time you finished the last volume of the *Foundation* trilogy and began *Foundation's Edge,* Psychology has come a long way in that period. Did you have to rethink the story because of psychology's progress?
Asimov: When I started *Foundation's Edge*, I had to rethink everything, and somehow it seemed that Hari Seldon's plan had become a little too primitive for me. I had to add additional refinements. First there was *Foundation* and *Second Foundation*, and both seemed to me insufficient, so I added a third group of people for further complications. I suppose this third group will be developed further in the fifth volume of the series, assuming that there is one.

I cannot honestly say that these additional complications that I introduced into *Foundation's Edge* are the result of my greater knowledge of psychology as compared with what I once knew. My formal training in psychology is nil, and my understanding of the subject may not go beyond common sense.

Kendig: What about biology? You received your Ph.D. in biochemistry in 1948, while you were still writing the original trilogy. Since then you have written a couple of dozen books and God knows how many articles on biological topics. Do you think an increased knowledge of the biochemistry of the brain will allow us to predict human behavior?

Asimov: I'm not certain. The brain is awfully complicated and it may well eventually come down to a decision as to whether a tiny nerve current is going to take one path or another. It is my understanding that every neuron in the brain is connected by synapses to a number of others. So the number of possible paths a nerve current can take is astronomically high. And the decision as to whether it's going to take one path or another might conceivably work its way down to the uncertainty principle. It might be balanced so exactly that even in principle you can't tell which path the current will take.

I wouldn't say that this is so. I don't know enough, but it may be that every last facet of human reaction is simply not predictable, even in principle. Which would be rather nice, because if the mechanism were complete— if total knowledge meant you could exactly predict what a human being will do—then we would be just extremely complicated robots.

Which perhaps we are. I have a feeling we will understand this better as we develop computers and robots. Perhaps when our computers reach an order of complexity similar to that of the human brain, we may find that they, too, get out of control in a way. It will be impossible then to predict completely what the robot or computer will do in response to a given stimulus. The same uncertainties that exist within the human mind may also exist within a computer's mind, which is not to say that the two would be identical. Merely that the complexities would be of the same level.

Kendig: In your robot stories you bring up the idea of machines out of control. You even devised three laws, the laws of robotics, to keep them in line. Well, computers are already reaching high levels of complexity. When do we have to start worrying? When do we have to build in the laws of robotics for our own safety?

Asimov: When they are so complex that we can't be sure of their responses. Then we'll have to put in generalized precautions, generalized safeguards. As long as what they do is precisely what we tell them to do, then we are the safeguards. But when they do not, then some kind of general guidelines will be necessary. I haven't the slightest idea how something like the three laws of robotics would be programmed into a computer, but I leave that to people who know more than I do.

Kendig: I gather that you are not paranoid about computers taking over.

Asimov: I'm not afraid of computers taking over. I think that is a simplistic idea. I don't see computers taking over any more than television sets are taking over or automobiles are taking over. I know that some people say that if computers are brighter than we are, then they may not need us. Well, automobiles go faster than we do, so they may not need us. The mere fact of being able to think better than we can is insufficient. Think in what way? Think how? It is foolish to think that all manner of thought is identical.

Computers are good at the manipulation of quantities, and they can do that faster than we can without error. They have always been able to. But human beings have insight, intuition, creativity—they are able to see connections that are not readily apparent. They can come up with surprisingly accurate answers from obviously incomplete information, and even the human beings themselves don't know where the answers came from.

One thing I do that strikes me as difficult for a computer to imitate is write stories. I know which incidents to tell first. I know when to break away from one scene and start another. I know which word is best to follow which word and I do it all very quickly and with very little conscious thought. I don't know how I would program a computer to write the way I do. I do it but I cannot explain how I do it. I have a computer on which I do word processing, and it does exactly what I tell it. But I can imagine a time when the computer word processor might be intelligent—it's intelligent enough now to point out when I've misspelled words, for instance, provided that the word is correctly spelled in its dictionary. If I use a word that is not in its dictionary, it tells me that no such word exists, and I ignore it. So no matter how smart it gets, it will never be smart enough to tell me how to write.

Kendig: What about privacy? Do you see a danger in computers knowing too much about us?

Asimov: I think that privacy, in a sense, is a nonissue. Privacy is a comparatively recent invention. In ancient times there was no such thing as privacy. You lived in very close quarters. Everyone knew everybody else's business. Today, in a place like New York, people have a certain amount of privacy not because they are hidden or protected, but because nobody gives a damn. The best guardian of privacy is to arrange your life so that you are a total bore and nobody wants to know about you.

Privacy vanished during World War II, when we decided to have high income taxes. The only way the government can get that much money out of people is to allow them reasonable exemptions—for business expenses, medical expenses, and so on. Well now, that is an open invitation for you to cheat, so the government has to be able to check up on you. I can't get a check from any magazine without telling them my Social Security number so they can report to the government that they paid me the money. I have to keep records and receipts in order to justify any deductions I take. I am assumed to be guilty unless I can prove my innocence, regardless of what the theory is. But to prove my innocence I must give up my privacy. Privacy is no defense. I cannot say to the government that it is none of their damn business, because that is not a recognized support for a deduction. Therefore, who cares? The battle is lost; it couldn't possibly be won.

Kendig: You mentioned that you now have a word processor. I think most of us thought that you had one all along—that or a team of writers chained in the basement. When did you get it and how has it changed the way you work?
Asimov: I got the computer in June of 1981. Before that, all of my books, novels or nonfiction, were written on a typewriter, then edited as lightly as possible, and retyped. So they went through the typewriter twice. The first drafts of my books are still written on the typewriter, but I don't edit. I take the draft exactly as it came out, put it on the desk next to my word processor, and edit it page by page on the computer until it's finished.

Kendig: So you use both a typewriter and a computer?
Asimov: For my books. For my short pieces, I use the word processor directly. I write a page, edit it, lock it in, and so on. Once I finish a page I don't make any further changes. I could, but it would mean having to learn more out of the computer's book of directions. I've learned the barest minimum required to do my work, and I'm hoping that I won't have to learn more.

Now, this is not necessarily engraved in stone. I may gradually use the word processor more and more. As a matter of fact, I did a small book, only 7,500 words, on the word processor because I knew in my head what the five chapters were going to be. I always write my books without any concern about chapters or sections within the chapters or anything like that. After I finish, I divide them up. To do that on the computer would require me to go to my instruction books.

Kendig: This may be a silly question, but what about your output? Are you writing more now that you have a computer?

Asimov: Well, it is sort of difficult to increase my output because, even in the old days before the word processor, I had reached a point where my speed of thought, my thinking, was the bottleneck. In other words, I turn out an essay just as fast as I can think it, and no matter how I improve the mechanics of getting it into the final form, I can't increase the speed of my thought any further.

However, if I typed the essay on my word processor and edited it there, I would gain some time. Then, instead of typing the final copy on the typewriter at ninety words a minute, my printer would type it at four hundred words a minute. So I save about three-quarters of the final typing time, about five-eighths of the total time of a short piece. And there are far fewer typos.

Kendig: An editor friend once told me that he found more errors and clumsier writing the further down a typewritten page he looked.

Asimov: Exactly. Many is the time I wanted to say, "The wind blew fiercely," and instead of an "f" typed an "h." And rather than cross it out, I wrote, "The wind blew horribly."

Kendig: There is a lot of research going on now in voice-actuated computers. Do you have any interest in a computer that you can talk to? Would you like to "speak" your books into the machine?

Asimov: I imagine that it's difficult to get executives to make use of the new computerized equipment because the process is associated with underlings. No matter how complex the computer may be, I have to give it instructions by typing and that is the work of an underling, by long tradition. It's the same with the telephone. Somehow, the act of dialing the number or pressing the buttons is déclassé for an executive. He says, "Ms. Jones, get me so and so," and she makes the call. And heaven help her if she gets another secretary and they have to fight about who gets on the telephone first, revealing a lower status. So to free the underlings for creative work, you have to be able to talk to the computer. And we should teach the computer to respond, "Yes sir, Dr. Asimov," in a properly deferential tone.

It would be nice if I could talk to the computer and have the words appear and then say, "No, dummy, cross that out!" But the problem is to get the computer to understand you. I'm not Laurence Olivier, and when I'm speaking quickly and my mind is distracted, I'm sure some of my words get swallowed.

The computer will have a job. It's easy for you because you're a human being. You take it as a whole. You can fill in the parts that don't make sense by saying "Now what's he trying to say?" and you'll get it right.

Kendig: I've read reports that the Japanese will have the first voice-actuated systems, since their language is more phonetic.
Asimov: Yes, we may have to develop a computer language that is a simplified version of English, one without the homonyms. For that matter, Spanish is a very phonetic language. There are no silent letters and no vowels with different pronunciations. Spanish might make a good computer language.

Kendig: You have done a lot of speculation and extrapolation, made predictions about the future. How have your predictions turned out?
Asimov: When I wrote the robot stories I had no thought that robots would come into existence in my lifetime. In fact, I would have bet they would not. But we do have robots, and furthermore, they are the kind I described—industrial robots, created by engineers to do specific jobs, with safeguards built in.

I was the first one—or the first one to get away with it—to portray robots in this way. The other stories written back in the 1940s, for the most part, showed robots as either menaces or symbols of a persecuted minority: Man invading the province of the Almighty to create a monster, or tales of a lovable robot put upon by cruel human beings. As a matter of fact, one of the leading manufacturers of robots today is a firm called Unimation. Joseph F. Engelberger, the president of Unimation, says he decided to devote his life to manufacturing robots after reading my robot stories. This is not my theory; he says so.

I also described a space walk quite accurately from a psychological standpoint back in 1952, which was about thirteen years before the first space walk actually took place. I said that it would give rise to feelings of euphoria and apparently that's what it did. Considering that I'm an acrophobe—I won't go into a plane and I don't see how you could force me to take a space walk—it pleases me that my imagination predicted correctly what a space walk would be like.

Kendig: Your *Foundation* series deals a lot with telepathy, mind communication; yet I know that you are extremely skeptical about the paranormal.

Asimov: Yes, I often deal with mental powers in my fiction and then spend a lot of my nonfiction dismissing them as utter nonsense and being very sarcastic at the expense of people who feel that there is something to them. There's a certain amount of schizophrenia there: I mean, I will do in my fiction what I simply will not allow in my nonfiction. I have written stories based on flying saucers, and I would have no hesitation writing a fictional story based on Immanuel Velikovsky's interpretation of solar-system history, even though I've spent essay after essay being sarcastic at Velikovsky's expense.

Kendig: Do you think there is danger in this kind of loose thinking—astrology, palmistry, that sort of thing? Is that why you're sarcastic?
Asimov: I think it's extremely dangerous because, for one thing, it destroys respect for science. Science is not something easy. There is no royal road to scientific discovery. The rules for evidence have to be strict, and to imagine that you can come up with important truths in the haphazard and foolish ways that fringe people invariably use is likely to vitiate science and all possibility of human advance.

I was at a conference once, discussing a television program that investigated a supposed perpetual-motion device without any attempt whatsoever to point out that by every law of thermodynamics this had to be wrong. The program left the impression that here at last was a device that would make energy out of nothing. A newspaper reporter said to me, "Well, it's just entertainment; what harm can it do?" And I said, "A great deal of harm." We live in a time when we are facing an energy crisis. It may be that millions, perhaps billions of lives will depend on our solving this crisis. Working out a system to replace the oil cannot be done overnight; we have to spend considerable time getting ready for it or else we'll be in serious trouble. And here we are spreading the news that there's no crisis at all because someone has discovered a way to make energy out of nothing.

Kendig: Would you call yourself an optimist? There seem to be a wave of new books out now with an optimistic leaning. I'm thinking of Herman Kahn and the Club of Rome people.
Asimov: If we're sane, then we have a bright future. We are at the edge of expanding into space and completely computerizing ourselves so that things are going to be amazingly different in the next century. If, on the other hand,

we are insane—if we spend all our money making war, or push the nuclear button, or refuse to take actions to solve our problems, then we might destroy ourselves. An unnecessary suicide. But I think there is a general tendency not to want to commit suicide, which is a hopeful sign. I think people are beginning to say that when it's really a matter of life and death, people will choose life. I think that's reflecting itself in the new books.

Kendig: Not long ago we asked a number of Nobel Prize winners what psychology might do for them, and what they, in turn, might do for psychology. In closing, I'd like to put the same question to you.

Asimov: What I would like from psychology is a better understanding of how individual human beings act, so that I can make my own novels more sensible. I have to make my characters act according to my own feel, my own intuition, which isn't good enough. I haven't studied people that well. I've lived a quiet and introverted life. I would like to see psychologists explain psychology a little more carefully than they have. I wish better maps were drawn. In terms of what I can do for psychology, I tend to look upon the world mechanistically. I don't want to suppose that there are problems that are inherent and insolvable. So in my *Foundation* series I invented what I call psychohistory, though I knew that it was entirely too simple to have real significance. But I would like psychologists to think about it. Are there rules of mob behavior? Could psychologists usefully study mob behavior or planetary behavior in such a way as to understand it better?—I hate to say to manipulate it better. To encourage it to be more social than anti-social?

I don't know, but I would like to see some psychologists at least thinking in that direction.

Isaac Asimov: Modern-Day Renaissance Man

Joy Walsh / 1984

From *The Humanist*, vol. 44 (July/August 1984). Copyright © 1984.

During the eighteenth century, around the time of *Dictionary*, Johnson's magnum opus of 1755, the ability of one man to have a firm grasp on the existing knowledge of the times ceased to be a possibility. Of his dictionary writing experience, Johnson states in the preface of that work: "Among those unhappy mortals is the writer of dictionaries; whom mankind have considered, not as the pupil, but the slave of science, the pioneer of literature, doomed only to remove rubbish and clear obstructions from the paths of Learning and Genius." Encyclopedic knowledge such as was possessed by Samuel Johnson would rarely be seen again due to the onslaught of scientific discovery and the speed with which it became disseminated.

Yet, down through the raging dynamos of time we have seen rare exceptions—rare Renaissance men who seem to possess near encyclopedic knowledge. This year's Humanist of the Year is just such a man. Isaac Asimov has mastered a great number of areas with more than two hundred and fifty books published in virtually every field of human knowledge. Of these, more than one hundred and twenty are on the sciences. It would take the mind of a Samuel Johnson or one of the encyclopedists of the *Encyclopedia Galactica of Terminus* to archive Asimov's writings.

In their book, *Humanism as the Next Step*, Lloyd and Mary Morain state that "Humanism . . . is the heir and creative fulfillment of the Renaissance." Renaissance thought can be defined as that period of transition from the medieval, theological to the modern, scientific interpretation of reality. Its emphasis is on humans and their place in the universe. "During the Renaissance," the Morains write, "there was a general rebirth of interest in the present, of zest for living."

Asimov's stand for the present, which reflects that humanistic Renaissance thinking, can be seen in his "Biographical Introduction" to *The Annotated*

"Gulliver's Travels," in which, after a discussion of *The Battle of the Books*, a book in which Swift develops his worship of the past, Asimov chides Swift: "For the force of his writing and the strength of his reasoning, the fact remains that Swift gazed back on the past and glorified it beyond its deserts while remaining willfully blind to the merits of the changing world which, in the end, continued to change without his permission and against his will."

Not only does Asimov's work embrace the future—it celebrates it. In the article, "Life on a Space Settlement," Asimov predicts humankind's marriage to outer space. Further, he predicts that "there will be nothing hidden; no more nooks to discover." When asked by the editor when all this would happen, Asimov states, "We already possess the technological capability. The difficulties are not so much a matter of technology as they are economical, political, and psychological." He then warns, "If human beings prefer to pay for deadly wars, to fight each other, and to cling in fright to Earth's surface, then we may never have space settlements."

Thus the mulish behavior of humans could indeed keep them nailed to a narrower and narrower future. Samuel Johnson's *Dictionary* defines the mule as an animal generated "between the he ass and a mare, or sometimes between a horse and a she ass." Shakespeare wrote often of the slavish aspects of the mule, but Pope's lines are more encouraging, "Twelve young mules, a strong laborious race." In Asimov's *Foundation Trilogy*, one of the great classics of science fiction, the character known as the Mule portrays a humanistic figure. He is the individualist, the freethinker, the one in control of his own mind.

The Mule is the one that the *Encyclopedia Galactica of Terminus* cannot define. His real name is unknown and his early life merely conjecture. We are told on page eleven of *Second Foundation*, that the Mule is "not germane to the issue at immediate hand." That the Mule defied the predictions of psychohistory is cause enough for him to be suspect in a world which would have a ruling class of psychologists.

Even though the Mule had miraculously reached the office of the First Citizen of the Union in a mere five years, he is destined to lose. The Mule, the poet mutant, would be destroyed not by power but by his own vulnerability and sensitivity in a world in which the universe becomes a deadly and hateful chess game. Of the Mule, it will be said by Stettin, his successor, "If there is any tradition in that world, it rests with the super-humanity and greatness of the Mule."

True, the Mule was a heretic who refused to accept Seldon's Plan to create a predictable world. As the *Encyclopedia Galactica* describes it, Seldon's Plan was "the synthesis of the calculus of n-variables and of n-dimensional geometry as the basis of what Seldon once called 'my little algebra of humanity.'"

Yes, we need our Mules—and our heretics. In *The Philosophy of Humanism*, Corliss Lamont sums up this need: "The study of history shows plainly how intense and unremitting have been religious, political, and social pressures upon those who have dared to challenge some traditional dogma and to blaze fresh paths through the jungles of human superstition."

With Isaac Asimov as Humanist of the Year, we have the tradition of the Renaissance man with us still in that his work, as Lamont states, "reveals a continuity with the vital humanist traditions of the Renaissance, as exemplified in its great artists and authors, and carries on their spirit in contemporary forms."

The Leading Edge
Victor Serebriakoff / 1984

From *Futures*, vol. 16 (August 1984): 435–43. Copyright © 1984.

This article is an edited version of a conversation between the Honorary President (Victor Serebriakoff) and the Honorary Vice President (Isaac Asimov) of Mensa International. This record of the historic conversation, held at the Rockefeller University, New York, represents a *tour d'horizon* of the most significant issues confronting the futures community.

Victor Serebriakoff: Where are recent advances going to have the most effect on tomorrow's world?
Isaac Asimov: In the first place, I would refer to the very rapid development of computers—the microchip, the developing wordprocessors, robots, even automobiles are becoming rapidly computerized. Every aspect of life is going to feel the effects of the computer very rapidly in the 1980s. Secondly, the change that will most affect us is going to be the advance into, and the exploitation of, space; almost every aspect of human life is going to take on new dimensions, because we are going to be out there.

VS: Turning to the question of the nuclear threat: the balance between offence and defence has been coming down more on the side of offence, but now people are beginning to talk about emerging technologies (ET) in the defence field, and the balance may be brought back more to the defensive side. How do you see the future in respect of this overwhelming threat of complete destruction?
IA: My belief is that the only adequate defence against nuclear warfare is not to have any. I think if the world population and the world's leaders were honestly to admit that nuclear war is unthinkable, they would destroy their nuclear weapons. I don't see how it is possible to live with the kind of nuclear armaments that a few nations have now, and to be sure that they won't be lured into using them. I don't think it could be limited if they are used—once

they are used, it will go all the way, and I suspect then that civilization will receive a blow from which it may well not recover.

VS: What about the "Star Wars" concept in defence—laser beams which could destroy nuclear missiles before they hit—do you think that is credible?
IA: I think enough missiles could be fired so that some would get through, and all it takes, really, is a few to start the ball rolling; this is not the sort of thing that I would care to take chances with.

VS: With regard to exponential change—people like Toffler seem to have become very frightened by the accelerating rate of change in human technology, ideas and institutions. There has never been such a long period of rapid progressive change. There have been plenty of periods of deleterious change. Exponential change is a worrying thing. I think there seem to be three possible things in this connection: this upsurge of the human spirit, this age of exploration, may, like others before it, disappear into an age of confusion. The second possibility is that somehow an exponentially increasing rate of change will continue without a disaster or complete change; and the third, of course, is that the world will return to a more stable state, or at least a diminished rate of change.
IA: I don't think that an exponential change, upward or downward, can long continue. If we have an exponential change upward, it will, in a surprisingly short time, outpace anything that we can conceivably do to keep up. I think that all experience shows us that exponential change reaches an inflection point, then levels off, until conditions change sufficiently so that there is a new period of exponential change.

VS: So you get the growth curve, then a plateau . . .
IA: And then a new growth curve under different conditions. I think that with earth as the only world on which human beings live, we are going to have to level off sooner or later, because the resources of earth are limited, its carrying capacity for human flesh and blood is limited. If we can expand into, and exploit, space, and establish settlements on other worlds, or build artificial space settlements, then we have a capacity for a new kind of exponential change. Even then, we can't expect to have an infinite number of human beings; population will still limit itself, although at a higher level. You would then have isolated cultural groups which can each proceed to change,

possibly in different ways so that the total would represent a new kind of expansion, not necessarily a unitary one, but a very multifarious one.

VS: You see them as symbiotic?

IA: They will be close enough so that they can always intercommunicate. On Earth, examples can be drawn from at least three different occasions in Western civilization. In Ancient Greece, there were hundreds of city-states spread over the different Greek lands, which went on developing their own customs, religious life and literature, with, in a sense, all benefiting and prospering from the richness of the culture they developed. Athens was by far the richest, but all the Greek city states contributed something. The second example was the Italian city-states of the Renaissance. And then in the nineteenth century the advance of science in Western Europe, for instance, was tremendously accelerated by developments in different nations—Germany at the time was a congerie of small nations, each with its own universities, each trying to be first in one way or another, so that there was again a kind of multifarious development of cultures. But now the advances of technology have arranged it so that earth shares a common science, shares a common business, shares in many ways a common culture.

VS: Why is it that these people who thought of themselves as competitive, fell into this symbiotic mode? We are brought up as competitive animals, most species are in at least limited competition with each other, but there seems to be some mysterious force that drives men into these large symbiotic congeries.

IA: Well, I suppose, to use Toynbee's phrase, eventually there develops a creative minority, a small group which is seen by others as having developed something that is so attractive that everyone wishes to adopt it. When Louis XIV built Versailles, this was so attractive a symbol of royalty and power that every principality in Europe built their own Versailles as far as they could afford it.

VS: Nothing in the biological history of the world leads us to expect this kind of imitativeness. Where do the values derive from so that the whole of mankind will suddenly turn to one thing?

IA: I suppose there are various ways in which this might happen. In our present culture, we much admire show-business personalities because they are defined as attractive. As far as accepting things from other cultures, the general population tends to be conservative, but the upper classes, who see themselves as part of a world culture, tend to adopt something they perceive as attractive, even though it may derive from another nation or another ethnic group.

VS: We have a world culture—a very large intercommunication network. Certain people in each culture are in parallel membership of the world culture and of their own—is that not a mysterious thing? The Soviet world is not cut off from it, it transcends all cultural and ideological differences.
IA: Well, there are vertical stratifications and horizontal stratifications. There are people in the U.S.A. with a thorough and intense education, and people who haven't had one. The educated people are perhaps interested in literature as a whole, in art, in science. The same is true all over the world. A person who is thoroughly educated and has taken to it well, and lives the intellectual life, does not feel much in common with people who have not had that education. If he were to be trapped with a number of them in a single room, he might be socially polite, but he would feel trapped. If he were in the same room with people on his level, who were from different nations, he might feel very much more at home than with his own compatriots who lacked his intellectual tastes.

VS: There is a considerable reaction against that world culture—for example, in Iran there is the rejection of the West, the return to a fundamentalist simple religious concept. People get frightened of this rate of change and turn back to what seems to us as inappropriate ideas. Do you feel that this resistance will gain strength?
IA: I don't think that the resistance could really succeed unless it ends in a nuclear war. As long as earth's culture survives, such resistances are sure to fail. The reason it arises of course is that one doesn't have an exact equality in all respects in the world culture. Modern technology is peculiarly the creation of North Western Europeans, and wherever it has progressed it has had to do so by being borrowed, and those who are less cosmopolitan and who value their own culture, sometimes resent it. However, I notice that they never resent it to the point of refusing it when they can see that it would not hurt them; for instance, the Iranian revolutionaries who wish to return their country to somewhere around AD 700, are nevertheless making full use of television.

VS: And modern weapons . . .

IA: They can't very well reject Western values that have any decent intellectual worth in order to accept these things that we create which are devilish and rotten.

VS: With regard to the communications explosion—the accelerating change has got a lot to do with the emergence of something which is biologically new in every possible way, namely, the enormous volume of information passing between nations all over the world. This is being much effected by computer connections: information is passing between computers all over the world in a way which is quite out of our control. Where do you see this international nerve net taking us? Will our governments find themselves helpless in possession of a system which knows what is going on better than they do?

IA: Back in 1949 I wrote a story asking this same question, of how the earth's economy was run by computers, and the earth's governments could not have control over the earth as they thought, since it was the computers that were running it. I am glad that I lived long enough to see my story no longer science fiction. I am firmly against computers in my personal life; I have resisted word-processors on principle.

I think that one of the remarkable changes which may be ahead of us in the future, aside from the fact that we are going to find that the controls will be unbudgeable, is that computers may completely alter our notions of education. In the past, no one was educated in the current, accepted sense, aside from learning their trade. Except for a small group amongst the aristocracy or amongst people who could enter the clergy, one person out of one hundred might learn to read and write, and get some inkling of the great thoughts of human beings. Then, with the invention of printing, and the availability of books, came the allure of literacy, and it was felt that everyone should have an education, especially since the industrial revolution made life complex to a point where people could not really run their own worlds unless they had learnt something. So we got the nineteenth century notion of a mass public free education where every child went to school, whether he wanted to or not, and had stuff rammed down his throat, whether he wanted it or not. It has never worked well, except that not doing it works even worse.

But now the question is, what is wrong with mass public free education? The answer, to my way of thinking, is that there is one teacher to every 30–50 students, which means that the 30–50 all have to be taught the same thing at the same time, and in general, very few of these students will find themselves learning what they want to learn, or at the rate that they want. In a sense, school is a very frustrating experience for everybody, and only a few people get as much out of it as they want to get out of it, if they just happen to be learning what they want to learn at the rate they can follow most comfortably. Once we have easily available computer information, where everyone can find out anything he wants to know, find out certain facts he wants, find out what people have written on a subject; he can in a sense guide his own education. School might become perhaps a series of signposts, indicating to him what he privately would like to follow up on his own, and he could endure school if it means once he gets home, he could proceed to educate himself along his own lines.

And if you have people able to learn what they want to learn, at the time they want to learn it, in the place they want to learn it, and at the speed they want to learn it, then I imagine education will become much more efficient. We will not only have a more educated world, but a more varied world, and one in which people are happier and more creative. I think that by making school as unpleasant as it is, and by making the learning process as unpleasant as it is, many people are imprinted with a life-long distaste for learning and education. They prefer ignorance.

VS: What will happen with the information explosion? It seems to have its own system of values. What do you see in the future from this growth of an intercommunications network, which is linking the world up spontaneously and not under any planned control? What will be the result?
IA: One feels initially that we will choke on all this information. Yet envisage the isolated small town where information is not a necessity, aside from for the local, parochial concerns. What we associate with these small towns of, say, the past century, before electronic communications, is an incredible avidity for information, where everybody sat around for endless hours, picked on thoroughly unimportant pieces of information and gossiped endlessly. Then, just as we find that there is now a great deal of information, we must also recognize the fact that the public really wants information. So I am not afraid of being too easily drowned by information, because all those old gossipmongers in the small towns never drowned in their endless gossip.

Second, most of the information is thoroughly evanescent. It is today's stock prices, which are outmoded tomorrow, to be replaced by tomorrow's stock prices. It is today's weather, today's sports scores, today's gold quotations, and material of this sort; even today's scientific theories may become nonsense tomorrow. I keep my *Scientific Americans*, but it is my experience that those of more than twenty years ago are strictly antiques, never to be referred to on pain of being poisoned by misinformation. So however rapid and copious the information becomes, if we talk about the information that is useful now it may not be so great. In addition, of course, different people are interested in different facets of information. It doesn't matter to me for instance, how rich and how copious the information on the financial pages are, I never look at them. It doesn't matter how copious the sports reports become, I never look at them either.

VS: There is, of course, the motor side, information which is really a set of instructions—you use information to make judgments and then actually carry them out. Much of the information which is flowing around in our computer systems in a thousand different channels is actually affecting things that happen. So these stock exchange results that you don't look at are nonetheless deciding what factories get built, what factories get torn down and which people get thrown out of work. The summation of the figure you don't read is having big social effects. This kind of information is taking over; the machine is running itself without the injection of human values at any point.

IA: I appreciate this point. A great many of the factors of my life are governed by the tax laws of the U.S.A. If the government changed the taxes in some way, I would change in response. On the other hand, the feeling that human values are ignored makes me wonder what human values are. Sometimes I feel that the true human values are greed and fear, and that this is what the computerization of the earth will respond to. Short-term profit with no look at long-term loss might finally govern us, because this is what we build into the computer. All over the world we have people grabbing for the next meal, grabbing for the next night's lodging, because they have to. And in that incredible lunge for short-term survival we ensure, perhaps, our long-term non-survival.

VS: Turning again to the question of education: now that there is the possibility of educating people in a much more simple, direct and individually attuned way, what future do we see for the currently existing enormous interlocked educational institutions? What will this new technology do to this cadre of the intelligent and educated, these members of the world culture, locked in to this worldwide skein of education institutions of various kinds.

IA: Obviously, if education changes, so will universities and research institutions. I feel that once people begin to educate themselves, by way of computerization, they will make missionaries of themselves. Every person who educates himself is not only a student, but also a potential teacher, and an intellectual missionary. There may be in this world a kind of explosion of creativity, as people try to make sure that their own interests are as widespread as possible; perhaps we might call it "intellectual imperialism." In a sense, the whole earth is likely to become a university. As to the actual physical structure that now supports the universities—perhaps we will have an upsurge of lecture halls and exhibition halls. Just as one particular use of a structure declines, another will arise. It is hard to look into the future and see it clearly.

VS: You say that people will follow their own interests, regardless of any possible social contribution they may make. But if that happens, there is going to be an increasing tendency for people to stop wanting to subsidize and pay for these institutions. There is no limit to the amount of things that man can see interest in and study in depth to find interesting theories about, but if they don't in the long run show some promise of contributing to human welfare, there is going to be a great reluctance to support dilettantist science. When education is offered more simply by computerized systems and so on, is that not a threat to the whole structure of the educational system; will it have to be supported out of private funds and private enthusiasm, rather than the state?

IA: There was a time in British history for instance, when the few aristocrats who had landed estates could rely on their world being run by their tenants and servants; they themselves could be dilettantes. My dream is of seeing the earth like that, when it is not unfortunate human beings of the lower classes who run it, but where computerized robots produce the necessary goods, where the population is carefully controlled, and where human beings are then, one and all, intellectual aristocrats, who can count on having the world run, leaving them to be creative. I am not sure that this is in the least bit possible, but it is my dream.

VS: A few of these dilettantes you mentioned produced world-changing modern science—a lot of them threw away their time.

IA: Early science was created by gentlemen—by people who did not have to worry about supporting themselves.

VS: With regard to world's consumable stores—many people are concerned with the rate at which energy and other irreplaceable materials are being used up. How do you see this problem—are we heading for an absolute disaster ecologically? There are those who think these problems will continue to be solved as they have been before.

IA: I agree that there have been problems of this sort before—there was an energy crisis, as a matter of fact, in the seventeenth century. Great Britain was largely deforested because it needed trunks of trees for the masts of their navy. The nation started using coal to burn, and this made the industrial revolution possible because it gave a large energy supply without destroying trees.

The feeling is that we will continue to find new energy sources—solar energy, hydrogen fusion and so on. The difference between the present energy crisis and the present environmental crisis and all earlier ones is that the stakes are higher now. The situation is, in a way, more unstable. We have far more human beings on earth to take care of, and we use energy at a far greater rate, so now we have less time to make the adjustment between energy supplies. Great Britain switched from wood to coal over the course of a century. Now we are liable to be faced with the necessity of switching from oil to other materials in the course of a decade.

Britain in the seventeenth century might well have gone into a state of temporary economic collapse, but affecting only around 2–3 million people; nowadays, if the world goes into an economic collapse, 4.5 billion people will be affected and even if only a small fraction of them die, it will be large in absolute numbers. So it is not the *nature* of the crisis, rather it is a world with hundreds of crises that bothers me.

The stakes are higher, the risks are greater, and we have got to act with more forethought and more diligence, and more concern for long-term events—it is becoming dangerous to grab for the short-term benefits. Sometimes we have to give up what seems to us to be there for the taking, in order that our grandchildren shouldn't find themselves without.

VS: Biological sciences—recent advances in the biological sciences have been as rapid as the advances in the physical sciences earlier in this century. Bio-engineering is becoming possible, mankind is beginning to promote its philosophy on biomorphic rather than mechanomorphic models. Great possibilities have been opened up—how do you view this?

IA: I suppose if you ask somebody who knows nothing about biology or genetic engineering what is going to become important in the biology of the future, they are likely to say clones. There is something magic about the word as it is seen by the average non-biologist. It bothers them, because they think on the one hand there is going to be an elite or on the other hand that there will be created a lot of poor quality people to use as cannon-fodder. Both are completely unlikely, because in neither case will genetic engineers work the way people think they do. On the one hand, why on earth use clones to create cannon-fodder, since the old, natural, system has already created it so effectively. The more serious question is whether we are going to be tempted to create large numbers of certain gifted or even just rich and privileged people to the expense of the common people. I also think that this is nothing to worry about, because there is more in a human being than his genes, there is also intra-uterine development and man's earlier social experiences.

VS: What I am thinking of is the possibility of creating food in vats, instead of in fields and throwing away 80 percent of produce, of being able to turn simple vegetable matter into complex proteins. This is beginning to happen: the engineering of this instruction belt, the genome, swapping bits and creating new species. Of course it is happening, at present, right down at the lower end of bacteria. With further development, that seems to offer the possibility of solving the food question completely. Won't this transform farming and transform our life completely?

IA: In the past, human beings have completely changed food habits.

VS: The green revolution is a recent example.

IA: Even before that, the invention of canning, and the invention of agriculture completely changed the world. Now I suppose it is possible that we might manufacture our food without regard to life, that it will be purely chemical.

VS: Would one use biological organisms to do this?

IA: People are developing inorganic catalysts for splitting the water molecule by means of the energy of visible light, essentially what choloro-phyll does—a kind of inorganic, man-made, artificial photosynthesis. From the hydrogen that is formed one can probably develop ways for creating starch and proteins and so on. We are still far from that now. Theoretically, we might be able to do this without the intervention of any life form; when we eat specific proteins, we don't care about their specificity, as long as the amino acids are there.

VS: And we could produce amino acids without biological processes?

IA: Well, some amino acids we can't produce, they have to be supplied in the diet, but if we have these amino acids in plenty, it doesn't matter what others we have. Let us stick to the microscopic life forms—some people might feel that we don't need to depend on other life forms for our food—this removes one of the constraints on our population. We could become many more times as populated, the world would consist only of people and tiny biologi-cal life forms, of human beings and their food. This would be a dreadful world—I have written stories on that too!

VS: You had better not write these stories—they come true too often!

IA: It would be nice if by manufacturing our own food by way of micro-scopic life forms and by controlling our population, we could remove the imbalance here on earth that has existed ever since the introduction of agri-culture—when we concentrated on producing those few plants and animals that we could eat, and called everything else weeds and vermin, and so began destroying the earth's ecology. I would like to see our independence of food make it possible for us to strengthen earth's ecology by turning over the land that we would no longer need to the wilderness.

VS: Finally, to the crucial question: what sort of long-term future ought we to be aiming for? What should the world be like in, say, a hundred years?

IA: The kind of world I would like to see is one in which the world's industry is lifted, to the largest extent possible, off the surface of the earth and put into space. We could then have what many people dream of—a pastoral world, free of those dark satanic mills. Yet they would be sited just a few thousand miles up, and we could still benefit from them, while they spew their pollution into outer space from which everything would be swept away into the outer solar system by the solar wind. Also I would like to see our microscopic forms of life, that are forming the carbohydrates and fats and proteins for us to eat, in large vats out in space where they can get all the energy of the sun, and where they can be purified and treated and sent back to Earth as food.

I would like to see people living in space, and having laboratories and observatories out in space. Perhaps earth itself will become the wilderness area, a pleasant place, a garden spot where people can go for vacations, where they can investigate Earth's ancient history, where they can see a large, incredibly complex ecology working out. Earth will be no longer the leading edge. It is out in space, in an expanding spatial civilization, which will be the leading edge. Earth will have achieved the retirement it so richly deserves.

From "Nightfall" to *Dawn*: Asimov as Acrophobe

Alan C. Elms / 1987

From *Extrapolation*, vol. 28 (1987): 130–39. Copyright © 1987. Reprinted by permission of Kent State University Press.

As a psychologist specializing in psychobiography, and as a science-fiction fan for over thirty-five years, I have become intrigued by the psychology of science-fiction writers. Why do they write, and why science fiction? How do their personalities relate to their work? What does writing science fiction *do* for them psychologically?

Sigmund Freud initially compared creative writing with neurotic symptoms. His later ideas about artistic creativity were much more complex, but creative writing is still most often characterized in the psychobiographical literature as serving a *defensive function* for the writer—simultaneously concealing and satisfying neurotic needs, or coping temporarily with repressed internal conflicts. In writing and teaching about science-fiction (and fantasy) writers, my favorite example for this psychological function has been Robert E. Howard. By writing about Conan and other superheroes who treat their women almost as savagely as their enemies, Howard managed for a time to keep the lid on his own problems with sex, aggression, and dependency needs. But he blew his brains out at age thirty, when his mother's impending death presented him with problems that storytelling could not resolve.

Writing fiction can also serve more psychologically healthful functions for the writer. In some cases it plays a valuable curative role in the writer's psychological functioning. The *restitutive function* of writing refers to the writer's effectively working through certain psychological problems during the process of writing—exploring his or her emotions, coming to understand at least symbolically the unconscious processes that have been causing personal difficulties, and learning to improve communication between various aspects of the writer's self while finding ways to bring similar insights to the reader. For psychological audiences, the example I use here is B. F. Skinner, who by writing his behaviorist utopia *Walden Two* (1948) was able to resolve serious identity problems, left over in part from a difficult adolescence. For science-fiction audiences, my favorite example of writing's restitutive function is Cordwainer Smith, who used his first bizarre stories to examine both his emotional pain and his intense need for psychological help. By the time he reached the mystical exhilaration of his final stories, Smith had gone through several kinds of psychotherapy. But his creation of a fictional universe probably helped him as much as any therapy did.

Not all writers begin with the extreme psychological problems of Robert E. Howard or Cordwainer Smith. For a writer with the usual range of psychological tics and quirks, the act of writing need not serve any major defensive *or* restitutive functions; it may simply be a means of self-expression. This *expressive function* is the one young writers often identify when asked why they write: "I want to express myself." Frederik Pohl has put it in more practical terms: "What a writer has to sell is his own perspective on the universe." It's a happy day when a writer discovers that written expressions of self not only can serve an expressive psychological function but can make money.

That brings up one other possibility: for some, writing may serve no psychological function at all, but is just another way to make a buck or to make an intellectual point. The latter may be especially true in science fiction, where ideas rather than strong emotions or violent acts often provide the focus for a story. Such writers may merely ring intellectual changes on previous work in the field, speculate on the long-range impact of recent or potential scientific discoveries, and work along as efficient wordsmiths rather than as self-therapists or even as self-expressers.

Early in my science-fiction research I looked for just such a writer, to contrast with Robert E. Howard and Cordwainer Smith. I wanted an example of a writer whose work displayed no psychological hangups and served no psychological functions but just told good stories. I first considered Robert Heinlein, but the obsessions of his later novels quickly disqualified him. Then I thought of Isaac Asimov—Asimov, the creator of simple characters and complicated science-fiction mysteries; Asimov, the genial popularizer of science; Asimov, enjoyed by everybody and psychologically disturbing to nobody. Surely Asimov was a clear contrast to the tormented Howard and Smith. Having read little of his fiction since my own adolescence, and knowing even less of his personal history, I found it easy to categorize Asimov as a writer whose work served no significant psychological functions for him.

Then my thinking about Asimov turned in a very different direction. The initial stimulus was his recent best-seller, *The Robots of Dawn*. I had read his first two robot novels, *The Caves of Steel* and *The Naked Sun*, when they were originally published. I remembered them fondly for their cleanly written, intellectually exciting combination of detection and robotics. I couldn't clearly recall either of the protagonists, human detective Elijah Baley or his robot partner Daneel Olivaw, and I didn't expect anything of great psychological interest in the new robot novel. I just hoped it would be as entertaining as the others.

I quickly discovered that much of *The Robots of Dawn* focuses not on the murder mystery and the interplanetary politics with which it is nominally concerned, but on Lije Baley's struggles to conquer his severe neurotic problems. Baley is agoraphobic (loosely, afraid of open spaces), acrophobic (afraid of heights), and phobic in several other ways. He can hardly leave his enclosed underground city without being overcome by panic. He experiences even greater difficulty when taking a routine spaceflight to another planet, as he must do in the course of his work. Here is the scene in which Baley approaches the planet Aurora in a spaceship:

The *ship* was moving. *He* was moving. He was suddenly aware of his own existence. He was hurtling downward through the clouds. He was falling, unguarded, through thin air toward solid ground.

His throat constricted; it was becoming very hard to breathe.

He told himself desperately: You are enclosed. The walls of the ship are around you.

But he sensed no walls.

He thought: Even without considering the walls, you are still enclosed. You are wrapped in skin.

But he sensed no skin.

The sensation was worse than simple nakedness—he was an unaccompanied personality, the essence of identity totally uncovered, a living point, a singularity surrounded by an open and infinite world, and he was falling.

Hmmm, I thought to myself as a psychologist, Isaac Asimov seems to know a lot about agoraphobic panic attacks—might he have problems along those lines himself? But I didn't think much more about the matter until several months later, when I went to my first Science Fiction Research

Association convention. Somebody there told me that both Ray Bradbury and Isaac Asimov had recently taken airplane rides for the first time in their lives. I already knew about Bradbury's fear of flying, and I'd heard that Andre Norton and several other science-fiction writers shared similar fears. I'd been amused by the apparent inconsistency of people who spend their creative lives writing about space travel and intergalactic wars but who fear boarding a plane for a hundred-mile trip. My amusement was restrained by my own uneasiness about flying—an uneasiness with which I often deal by marching onto a plane and quickly losing myself in a science fiction novel.

Now I began to consider *The Robots of Dawn* in the light of Asimov's reported airplane ride. Suppose Isaac Asimov himself suffers from really intense agoraphobia or acrophobia or both. (Clinically they're not far apart, and Lije Baley suffers from both in the robot novels.) Suppose Asimov has been struggling to overcome his severe agora- and/or acrophobia for many years, just like his hero Baley. Suppose he has used his writing of science fiction to work through his severe emotional problems, perhaps with a psychotherapist's help, just like Cordwainer Smith. Suppose he has finally conquered his phobia(s), has boarded a plane, and taken off. Another triumph for the psychological restitutive powers of writing science fiction!

On the basis of that interesting hypothesis, I began to gather data on Asimov. First I reread his earlier robot novels. Lije Baley's agoraphobia, I found, was not only named and described in both books but was specifically identified by Asimov with a fear of flying (e.g., *The Caves of Steel* and *The Naked Sun*). I also checked several of Asimov's short stories written at about the same time. I quickly discovered a whole series of stories about another interplanetary detective, Dr. Wendell Urth, whose travel anxieties are so extreme that he "had never in his adult life been more than an hour's-walk from his home on the University campus" (*Asimov's Mysteries*).

Then I moved on to even earlier works, especially Asimov's first major short story, "Nightfall," published in 1941 and now widely regarded as the best science-fiction story ever written. "Nightfall" is an ironic answer to Emerson's rhetorical question, "If the stars should appear one night in a thousand years, how would men believe and adore, and preserve for many generations the remembrance of the city of God?" Asimov's story describes the inhabitants of the planet Lagash, whose six suns give them perpetual sunlight—except for once every 2,049 years, when all the suns simultaneously set or go into eclipse. When that happens, all the Lagashians promptly go stark-raving mad. Their madness, according to the story, comes from intense claustrophobia, the exact opposite of Asimov's apparent problems. But as the story ends, claustrophobic *and* agoraphobic anxieties appear to mix: the Lagashians react with terror not only to seeing the entire sky get as dark as a cave, but also to experiencing the vastness of the universe for the first time when the stars emerge. This odd mixture suggested to me that in trying to depict the claustrophobic insanity of the Lagashians, Asimov had drawn upon his own agoraphobic anxieties to get a feel for what it must be like to go mad.

Next I looked at Asimov's massive autobiography. There he refers several times to what he calls his "severe acrophobia," e.g.: "I was afraid of heights and went out of my mind at the sensation of falling" (*In Memory Yet Green*). He also describes his negative experiences with roller coasters; his two brief and uncomfortable rides in military planes during World War II, apparently never repeated; and his strong preference for enclosed spaces. Asimov doesn't use the technical term for such a preference in his autobiography, but he knows it; in *The Robots of Dawn*, a character from a distant planet refers scornfully to "the claustrophilia of you Earthmen, your dislike of leaving your walls." The author is clearly describing his own claustrophilia there. As Asimov puts it in his autobiography, "Why it should be, I don't know, and psychiatrists may make what they like of it (for I will not ask them, and I will not listen if they try to tell me), but I have always liked enclosed places."

Actually Asimov does know something about "why it should be." In his autobiography he supplies the beginnings of an explanation at least for his fear of flying, and by inference for his pleasure in enclosed spaces. He says he had to "bear the brunt of his parents' neuroses," and continues: "My parents—my mother, especially—trembled over my well-being so extremely, especially after my babyhood experience with pneumonia, that I couldn't help but absorb the fear and gain an exaggerated caution for myself. (That may be why I won't fly, for instance, and why I do very little else that would involve my knowingly putting myself into peril)."

I went from Asimov's autobiography to James Gunn's very thoughtful monograph, *Isaac Asimov: The Foundations of Science Fiction*. I found that Gunn had dealt specifically with the intertwined themes of "claustrophilia and agoraphobia" in the first two robot novels. He writes, for instance, "Finally . . . *The Naked Sun* is about Elijah Baley and his battle against agoraphobia." On the basis of extensive interviews Gunn adds that Asimov "would say that it doesn't matter how the past has shaped him. He is satisfied to be what he is: a claustrophile, an acrophobe, a compulsive writer."

Finally, as a conscientious psychobiographer should always do when studying a live subject, I wrote to Asimov himself. In my first letter I referred to H. L. Gold, the founding editor of *Galaxy*, whom Asimov had described in his autobiography as being extremely agoraphobic. I said I assumed that Asimov wasn't as agoraphobic as Gold, but that Elijah Baley certainly had lots of problems with agoraphobia in the robot novels, and so did some of Asimov's other fictional characters. Then I boldly asked:

Is Baley's agoraphobia in any sense an exaggerated version of your own feelings at being out in the open rather than in an enclosed environment? Have Baley's struggles to overcome or cope with such feelings reflected your own attempts to come to terms with agoraphobic or acrophobic feelings? If so, have you been successful (or how much have you been successful) in your efforts—either through writing fiction that deals with these issues, or through other means of dealing with them? Or have you simply used your own experiences as a starting-point for developing a characterization of Baley and others, without making any strong efforts to deal psychologically with feelings that you can deal with more effectively in other ways (such as spending most of your time in a comfortable room without open windows)? Finally . . . somebody told me you had recently taken your first plane ride in many years. If that's true, was that the result of some recent resolution of your agoraphobic or acrophobic feelings, or was it merely a matter of circumstance?

Asimov responded by return mail from his Manhattan apartment:

Baley's agoraphobia was, perhaps, my way of getting back at Gold for forcing me to do a robot novel, but I do have agoraphobic tendencies myself. Very mild, of course. I prefer enclosed places to open places but only to the extent that I prefer coffee to tea. My typewriter and library are in two rooms in which the blinds are always down. My word-processor, however, is in the living room, where one whole wall, virtually, is glass (and 33 stories up) and where my wife likes to have the sun (or clouds) streaming in. So I work on the word-processor without complaint and without trouble. Again, when I walk through Central Park I prefer to stick to the paths, rather than walk over grass and given my own choice I would prefer to walk around it. I feel comfortable in the canyons of Manhattan, but I will walk across empty spaces if I have to.

My acrophobia is much more severe. I live on the 33rd floor and I don't mind looking out the window horizontally, but I would be very uncomfortable looking *down* and I rarely try it. We have two balconies and I can get out upon them if there is some reason to do it, but I rapidly get uncomfortable and go back in.

However, my writing is certainly not a conscious attempt to deal with this. I feel no need to deal with it. I don't mind being acrophobic since I have no desire whatever to go up in a plane or to climb a mountain or to walk a tightrope.

As for the airplane, that wasn't I. It was Ray Bradbury who finally took an airplane and made the newspapers in so doing. I am made of sterner stuff and feel no urge to go through the kind of travelling that will put me in an airplane. In fact, I have no urge to do *any* kind of travelling. Left to myself, I would be perfectly content to stay on the island of Manhattan for the rest of my life. And when I do leave, it is only for short distances, and I return as soon as I can. . . . [P]lease let me impress upon you the fact that I am happy with myself exactly as I am and I am spending my life *exactly* the way I want to spend it. [His emphases.]

So much for my idea that Asimov may have been making his fiction serve a restitutive psychological function. As he presented matters in the letter, he seemed to be ruling out even a defensive function: he insists that his agoraphobia is very mild, his acrophobia doesn't bother him because he's organized his life to avoid dangerous high places, and he doesn't need to use his writing to deal with anxieties because he's really quite happy. Being a psychologist, I felt a little dubious about the latter argument. But I was willing to entertain the possibility that Asimov's writing serves mainly an expressive function rather than an anxiety-reducing one. I was also interested in Asimov's intimation that he had modeled Baley's agoraphobia mainly on Horace Gold's severe case rather than on Asimov's milder version. Here was a psychological function of creative writing that I had not previously considered—a passive-aggressive function, a psychology of revenge against obnoxious editors.

When I wrote to Asimov again, I asked whether he had *consciously* made Baley agoraphobic in order to get back at Horace Gold, or whether he only later realized that Baley's character evolved in that direction because Asimov was unconsciously resentful of Gold's editorial demands. I also mentioned the odd combination of agoraphobic and claustrophobic panic in the short story "Nightfall," and said, "You probably don't remember the details of story composition after so long a time (though I've often been impressed by how much you do remember), but I'd be interested to know, for instance, whether you had read any psychological works before writing "Nightfall" that might have given you some ideas about how to depict the characters' fears." Asimov again responded promptly:

> First, about Baley's agoraphobia.
>
> That I was influenced by Gold's agoraphobia is undoubted. That was the thing that was most noticeable about Horace and when I wrote the novel we were at our closest. That I was unconsciously resentful of Horace's demands and took vengeance by making Baley agoraphobic is a later bit of self-analysis. I have no way of proving this was so. There were times when my resentment of Horace became conscious and pronounced but this was not because of his driving me to write specific things but because his rejections were bitterly vituperative. . . .
>
> Secondly, about the reactions in "Nightfall."
>
> That was 44 years ago and it is difficult even for me to reconstruct the situation. . . . I am myself not afraid of the dark (and never was) and am not in the least claustrophobic so it interested me to *pretend* claustrophobia in my own mind and try to imagine what it was like. As for the fear of the stars or the sky, that was a "given" in the story when [*Astounding* editor John W.] Campbell and I discussed it. We had to reverse Emerson's thesis, so I had no choice there. I did *not* read psychological works before "Nightfall," or after either. I am illiterate in psychology to this day. When any of my stories introduce what seem to be psychological insights, they are either picked up in general reading, or in observation, or in my own very lively imagination. [His emphases.]

In addition to my specific inquiries about the robot novels and "Nightfall," my second letter had included a more general paragraph, added hesitantly and phrased tentatively because I was not sure how far Asimov's tolerance of my questions would extend:

> I appreciate your feeling that you're happy with yourself and that you're spending your life just the way you want to spend it. . . . But let me raise the question, for the sake of argument—and I think I do need to raise it in my paper, before somebody else raises it for me: May you not be just being defensive, denying your anxieties by avoiding introspection and by writing vast amounts of material that divert your and others' attention away from some kind of underlying uneasiness or self-doubt? I suppose that question represents the stereotypical psychoanalytic assumption,

with which I do not necessarily agree, that everybody is neurotic *somehow* but that not everybody realizes it. Do you have a response to that that satisfies you, if not the psychologists and psychiatrists who might ask it?

Asimov responded:

> Finally: Honestly, I am not defensive. I am a genuinely happy person except where the outside world impinges—if I develop clogged coronaries and am threatened with death, if those I love are unhappy for good reason, etc. When unthreatened by the outside and left entirely to my own devices, I am openly happy. The fact is I write easily, I receive instant appreciation for my work, I make a good living, my wife and daughter love me, I have good and affectionate friends—I have no *reason* for unhappiness. And in my whole life I have never had self-doubt. I have known exactly what I could do from the very start and I have gone out and done it. [His emphasis.]

Until those last two sentences, I felt willing to give Asimov the benefit of the doubt. After all, he knows firsthand whether he's happy or not, whether he's anxious or not, and he has a lot more information about his own psychological state than I do. But never any self-doubt? Asimov himself once wrote that when he made his second *Galaxy* sale to Horace Gold, "a more-than-seven-year agony of self-doubt was relieved" (*Nightfall*). Is it really true, as Asimov asserted in his letter, that he has known exactly what he could do from the very start and has gone out and done it? Not if we can judge from the voluminous evidence of his autobiography. Is he being totally honest with himself, and genuinely undefensive, when he says, "Honestly, I am not defensive. I am a genuinely happy person. . . . I have no *reason* for unhappiness"? Well, as the narrator in Asimov's mystery novel *Murder at the ABA* puts it, "The super-secure are never secure."

Now, I realize that nothing is more likely to put a person on the defensive than a psychologist asking, "Are you being defensive?" So maybe Asimov was just overreacting a bit to my questions when he said he'd never felt any self-doubt and so on. Maybe in less defensive moments he would again admit to occasional self-doubts and to intermittent moments of unease among all the happiness. I would grant in turn that as he now lives his life, mostly indoors and mostly in front of his word-processor keyboard, Isaac Asimov probably *is* one of the world's happier people. But I am not going to use him any more as an example of a writer whose work serves no significant psychological function.

Rather, I suspect that his work serves all three functions for him. Asimov's case is surely more complicated than I initially assumed, and a detailed functional analysis will require a much more thorough study of his fiction and his autobiography than I or anyone else has yet done. But the evidence considered here suggests that Asimov's style of life and his writing have been simultaneously shaped by a creative engagement between his talents and his fears. His writing has clearly served an important *expressive* function for him; anyone who has read a few of his editorial introductions to other people's stories will know how much Asimov enjoys being Asimov in print. His writing has served important *defensive* functions, the dimensions of which are not yet clear; among other things, his exaggeration of his own phobias in his fictional protagonists may have helped him live more comfortably with his modest anxieties. And his writing has probably served significant *restitutive* functions over the years, though he denies any "conscious attempt" to work in that direction. He may not have mastered all his anxieties, but the self-exploration entailed in his long writing career must have figured importantly in the evolution of the sensitive, caring individual evident in much of his recent work.

In response to direct questioning, Asimov may continue to deny that his writing serves *any* of these functions. But once again, he has already put himself on record, acknowledging the three functions—less clearly differentiated than I would like, but definitely all there—in one of his not altogether tongue-in-cheek autobiographical notes (*Nightfall*): "The niceness of being a writer, of course, is that you can take all your frustrations and annoyances and spread them out on paper. This prevents them from building up to dangerous levels and explains why writers in general are such lovable, normal people and are a joy to all who know them."

Isaac Asimov Speaks

Bill Moyers / 1988

From *The Humanist*, vol. 49 (January/February 1989). Copyright © 1989. Reprinted by permission of Bill Moyers.

There's something so clean, so compelling, so definite about the coming year 2000 that everyone, it seems, is indulging in a little millennial enthusiasm. But consider this: that same year in the Byzantine calendar will be called 7507 and in the Jewish calendar, 5759. The Chinese will be marking the year 4698, and it will be the year 1418 in the Mohammedan calendar. Those calculations come from a man who is famous for thinking globally and rationally. He tells us why we all must follow suit if we want to survive and why we can't wait for the year AD 2000 to start.

Isaac Asimov. Whatever you've read, you've probably read something of his. Science fiction, of course—his Foundation series is a classic—science fact, chemistry, astronomy, physics, biology. Children's books. History. Math. One scientist calls him "the greatest explainer of the age." The American Humanist Association has named Dr. Asimov the Humanist of the Year. And some religious folk have considered him the incarnation of the devil.

This past October, in the Great Hall of Cooper Union in New York City, where Americans have been debating ideas since the days of Abraham Lincoln, I asked Dr. Asimov about his faith in the power of human reason.

—Bill Moyers

Bill Moyers: Are you an enemy of religion?

Isaac Asimov: No, I'm not. I feel, as it seems to me any civilized, humane person should feel, that every person has the right to his own beliefs and his own securities and his own likings. What I'm against is attempting to place a person's belief system onto the nation or the world generally. You know, we object because we say constantly that the Soviet Union is trying to dominate the world, communize the world. But I certainly would be very much against trying to Christianize the world or to Islamize it or to Judaize it or anything of the sort. And my objection to fundamentalism is not that they are fundamentalists but that essentially they want me to be a fundamentalist, too.

Now, I can imagine they object. They say I believe that evolution is true, and I want everyone to believe that evolution is true. But I don't want everyone to believe that evolution is true. I want them to study what we say about evolution and decide for themselves. Now, they say they want to teach creationism on an equal basis. But they can't. It's not a science. You can create creationism in the churches, in the courses on religion. I mean, they would be horrified if I would suggest that in the churches they teach secular humanism as an alternate way of looking at the universe or that they teach evolution as an alternate way of considering how life may have started.

In the church, they teach only what they believe. And rightly so, I suppose. But on the other hand, in schools, in science classes, we've got to teach what scientists think is the way the universe works.

BM: But, of course, this is what frightens many, many believers. They see science as uncertain, always tentative, always subject to revisionism. They see science as a complex, chilling, and enormous universe, ruled by chance and impersonal laws. They see science as dangerous.

IA: That is really the glory of science—that science is tentative, that it is not certain, that it is subject to change. What is really, in my way of thinking, disgraceful is to have a set of beliefs that you think is absolute and has been so from the start and can't change—where you simply won't listen to evidence. You say, "If the evidence agrees with me, it's not necessary. If it doesn't agree with me, it's false."

This is the legendary remark of Omar when they captured Alexandria and asked what to do with the library. He said, if the books agree with the Koran, they are not necessary and may be burned. If they disagree with the Koran, they are pernicious and must be burned.

Well, there are still these Omar-like thinkers who think that all of knowledge will fit into one book called the Bible and refuse to allow that there is even the conceivability of an error in there. That, to my way of thinking, is much more dangerous than a system of knowledge which is tentative and uncertain.

BM: Do you see any room for reconciling the two world views: the religious, the biblical view, the universe as God's drama, constantly interrupted and rewritten by divine intervention; and the universe as scientists hold it, always having to be subjected to the test of observation and experimentation? Is there any room for reconciling?

IA: Well, there is if people are reasonable about this. There are many scientists who are honestly religious. You can rattle off the names of them, Milliken was a truly religious man; Morley, of the Michelson and Morley experiment, was truly religious. There are hundreds of others who did great scientific work, good scientific work, and at the same time were religious.

But they did not mix their religion and science. In other words, they did not presume that if something they didn't understand took place in science they could dismiss it by saying, "Well, that's what God wants," or, "at this point a miracle took place." No, they know that science is strictly a construct of the human mind working according to the laws of nature and that religion is something that lies outside and may embrace science.

On the one hand, you know, if there were some need to arise evidence—scientific, confirmable evidence—that God exists, then we'd have no choice; scientists would have no choice but to accept that fact. On the other hand, the fundamentalists don't admit the possibility of evidence, let us say, that would show that evolution exists, because any evidence you present they will deny if it conflicts with the word of God as they think it to be. Therefore, the chances of compromise are only on one side, and I doubt that it will take place.

BM: If God is dead, everything is permitted. That's what scares them.
IA: Well, on the contrary. They assume that human beings have no feeling about what is right and wrong. Is the only reason you are virtuous because that's your ticket to heaven? Is the only reason you don't beat your children to death because you don't want to go to hell? It seems to me that it's insulting to human beings to imply that only a system of rewards and punishments can keep you a decent human being. Isn't it conceivable that a person wants to be a decent human being because that way he feels better? Because that way the world is better?

I don't believe that I'm ever going to heaven or hell. I think that when I die there will be nothingness. That's what I firmly believe. That does not mean that I have the impulse to go out and rob and steal and rape and everything else because I don't fear punishment. For one thing, I fear worldly punishment. And for a second thing, I fear the punishment of my own conscience. I have a conscience. It doesn't depend on religion. And I think it's so with other people, too.

Besides, even in societies in which religion is very powerful, there's no shortage of crime and sin and misery and terrible things happening—despite heaven and hell. I imagine if you go down death row where a bunch of murderers may be waiting for execution and ask them if they believe in God, they'll tell you yes.

BM: Is there a morality in science?

IA: Oh, absolutely. There is a morality in science that is further advanced than anywhere else. If you can find a person in science, and it happens—scientists are only human—who has faked his results, who has lied as far as his findings are concerned, who is trying to steal the work of another, who has done something scientists consider unethical, his scientific reputation is ruined, his scientific life is over, and there is no forgiveness.

BM: Because the morality is . . . ?

IA: The morality is that you report the truth. And you do your best to disprove your own findings. And you do not utilize someone else's findings and report them as your own. In any other branch of human endeavor—in politics, in economics, in law, in almost anything—people can commit crimes and still be heroes. Somehow, to my way of thinking, for instance, Colonel North has done terrible things. Yet, he's a hero and a patriot to some people.

And this goes on in almost every field. Only science is excepted. You make a misstep in science and you're through—really through.

BM: You love the field, don't you? You love science.

IA: Oh, I'm very fond of it. I think that it's amazing how many saints there have been among scientists.

I'll give you an example. In 1900, DeVries studied mutations. He found a patch of evening primrose of different types, and he studied how they inherited their characteristics. And he worked out the laws of genetics. Two other men worked out the laws of genetics at the same time: Charles Carrinse, who was a German—DeVries was a Dutchman—and Eric von Chermark, who was an Austrian. All three worked out the laws of genetics in 1900. All three looked through the literature just to see what had been done before. All three discovered that in 1867 Gregor Mendel had worked out the laws of genetics, and people hadn't paid any attention then. All three reported their findings as confirmation of what Mendel had found. Not one of the three attempted to say that it was original with himself, once he had discovered Mendel's work. And that's the sort of thing you just don't find outside of science.

You know what it meant? It meant that two of them—Carrinse and Chermark—lived in obscurity and that DeVries is known because he also was the first to work out the theory of mutations. But as far as the discovery of genetics is concerned, Mendel gets all the credit. And they knew at the time that this would happen, but they did it.

BM: It is the truth that excites you. So what is the value of science fiction, for which you are justifiably universally known?
IA: I think that serious fiction, fiction where the writer feels he's accomplishing something besides simply amusing people—and there's nothing wrong with simply amusing people—is holding up a mirror to the human species. He's making it possible for you to understand people better because you've read the novel or story—maybe making it possible for you to understand yourself better. This is an important thing.

Now, science fiction uses a different method for doing this. It works up an artificial society—one which doesn't exist, one which may possibly exist in the future but not necessarily—and it portrays events against the background of this society. It's amusing; it's interesting. And one hopes that it will give a new way of looking at people and looking at yourself—that you will see yourself seen against the strange society in ways you couldn't possible see yourself seen against the present society.

I don't claim that I succeed in this. It seems to me that to do this properly takes a great man, one on the level of, well, at least half of, Shakespeare. And I don't come up there. But I try, and who knows, maybe once in a while I succeed a little bit. But I try. And that's why I write science fiction, because it's a way of writing fiction in a different style and enables me to make points I can't make otherwise.

BM: Someone said that one great advantage of science fiction is to introduce the reader to the idea of change—changes that may well be inevitable but which are not conceivable to the reader.
IA: Well, I've said that myself at different times. The fact is that society is always changing, but the rate of change has been accelerating all through history for a variety of reasons. One thing, change is cumulative. The very changes you make make it easier to make further changes.

It was only with the coming of the Industrial Revolution that the rate of change became fast enough to be visible in a single lifetime, so that people were suddenly aware that not only were things changing but they would continue to change after they died. And that was when science fiction came into being, as opposed to fantasy and adventure tales, because people knew that they would die before they could see the changes, to what happened in the next century. So it would be nice to imagine what they might be. And other people decided to make money that way.

As time goes on, the rate of change still continues to accelerate. It becomes more and more important to adjust what you do today with the fact of change in the future. It's ridiculous to make your plans now on the assumption that things will continue as they are now. You'll have to assume that, if something you're doing is going to reach fruition in ten years, within those ten years changes may take place and perhaps what you're doing will have no meaning then.

So nowadays, futurism has become an important part of thinking in business, in economics, in politics, in military affairs. At any rate, science fiction is important because it fights the natural notion that people would have that somehow there's something about things the way they are right now which is permanent.

BM: Use your imagination, which you do so often, in this way. If the next president asks you to draft his inaugural address and says, "Dr. Asimov, make sure I say the one thing you think I must convince the American people that they should pay attention to," what would it be?
IA: It would be this: that all the problems we face now that are really important for life and death are global problems—that they affect all of us alike. The ozone layer, if it disappears, disappears for all of us. Pollution in the ocean, in the atmosphere, in the ground water, affects all of us. The only way we can ameliorate these problems, solve them, prevent them from destroying us, is again a global solution. We can't expect that anything the United States alone does is going to affect the situation the world over. There's got to be cooperation among the nations of the world. International cooperation is absolutely essential.

BM: What about the one subject you've written so much about: the population explosion—you know, the fact that right now the population of the globe is over five billion. You've said that, if it continues at its 2 percent growth rate a year, it will be what in another—

IA: Well, actually, it's down to 1.6 percent, but with a higher population it's the same amount in actual numbers: 80 million a year. Therefore, by the year 2000, it's going to be perhaps 6.5 billion.

BM: That's just twelve years from now.
IA: Yes, it's going up very fast.

BM: How many people do you think Earth is able to sustain?
IA: I don't think it's able to sustain the five billion in the long run. Right now, most of the world is living under appalling conditions. And we can't possibly improve the conditions of everyone. We can't raise the entire world to the average standard of living in the United States, because I don't think we have the resources and the ability to distribute well enough for that. We have condemned, right now as it is, most of the world to a miserable starvation-level existence. And it will just get worse as the rate of population continues to go up.

BM: But you just can't say to a woman, "Don't have children."
IA: Well, you know, it's not so much that. It's so many people are saying, "Have children." There is such a pronatalist attitude in the world. We celebrate Mother's Day so enthusiastically. We say, "May all your troubles be little ones." We celebrate additional children. I feel sometimes that if we'd only stop pushing for children that somehow there'd be fewer of them.

BM: Why did you say that the price of survival is the equality of women?
IA: Because if women have full ability to enter into all facets of the human condition—if they can enter business, if they can enter religion, science, government—on an equal basis with men, they will be so busy that they won't feel it is necessary to have a great many children. As long as you have women under conditions where they don't feel any sense of value—no self-worth except as mothers, except as baby factories—they'll have a lot of children, because that's the only way they can prove they're worth something.

In general, if you look throughout the world, the lower the status of women, the higher the birth rate. And the higher the birth rate, the lower the status of women. So then, if you could somehow raise the status of women, I am certain the birth rate will fall drastically through the choice of the women themselves.

BM: What do you see happening to the idea of dignity to human species if this population growth continues at its present rate?

IA: It's going to destroy it all. I use what I call my bathroom metaphor. If two people live in an apartment and there are two bathrooms, then both have what I call freedom of the bathroom—they can go to the bathroom any time they want and stay as long as they want for whatever they need. To my way of thinking, this is ideal. Everyone believes in the freedom of the bathroom. It should be right there in the Constitution. But if you have twenty people in the apartment and two bathrooms, no matter how much every person believes in freedom of the bathroom, there is no such thing. You have to set up times for each person, you have to bang on the door, "Aren't you through yet?" and so on.

And in the same way, democracy cannot survive overpopulation. Human dignity cannot survive it. Convenience and decency cannot survive it. As you put more and more people onto the world, the value of life not only declines but disappears. It doesn't matter if someone dies.

BM: Of course, so many people say that the United States is bringing its population under control, that we're going to have a stable population, that we're not even reproducing ourselves, and that what the rest of the world does we can't control.

IA: The population of the United States is still going up. The only time it went up really slowly was during the Great Depression. There were no laws sort of lowering the birth rate; there was just an economic depression, which made people think twice before they had children.

But the United States is doing something else, which is absolutely refusing to help other nations control population. Our feeling is somehow that it's enough for us to somehow make sure that the United States is in good shape and that what other nations do is their business. It's not just their business; it's our business, too.

BM: In other words, we can't exist as a stable economy when around us is turmoil, chaos?

IA: Absolutely not. Right now in many nations they're just destroying the rain forests because they need the firewood, they need the space for farms.

BM: Why should I care about that?

IA: Because without the rain forests, we're going to have deserts instead. The food supply will dwindle. As a matter of fact, there's even the possibility that we're going to lose all kinds of valuable substances we know nothing about. Those rain forests have an incredible number of species of plants and animals that we know very little about. Some of them may produce chemicals of great importance pharmacologically and medically. Some of the plants might, if properly cultivated, be new food sources. And in addition to that, nothing produces the oxygen of the atmosphere with the same intensity that a forest does. Anything that substitutes for it will be producing less oxygen. We're going to be destroying our atmosphere, too.

BM: You've lived through a lot of this century. Have you ever seen human beings think with the perspective you're calling on them to think with now?

IA: Well, it's perhaps not important that every human being thinks so. How about the leaders thinking so? How about the opinion-makers thinking so? Ordinary people might follow them if we didn't have leaders who are thinking in exactly the opposite way; if we didn't have people who are shouting hatred and suspicion of foreigners; if we didn't have people who are shouting that it's more important to be unfriendly than to be friendly; if we didn't have people shouting somehow that people inside the country who don't look exactly the way the rest of us look, that something's wrong with them. Again, it's almost not necessary for us to do good. It's only necessary for us to stop doing evil, for goodness sake.

BM: Do you think that we can educate ourselves? That any one of us, as you once said, at any time, can be educated in any subject that strikes our fancy?

IA: Well, the key words there are "that strikes our fancy." There are some things that simply don't strike my fancy, and I doubt that I can force myself to be educated in them. I have never really been interested in economics, for instance, or in psychology or in art as a nonspectator—to really know what art is all about. And, therefore, even if I try to read about it, it bounces off. On the other hand, when there's a subject I'm ferociously interested in, then it is easy for me to learn about it. I read it. I absorb it. I take it in gladly and cheerfully. I've written more books on astronomy than on any other science, and no one has ever complained that my astronomical books are wrong, silly, or anything like that. I've never taken a course in astronomy.

I'm completely self-trained in it. On the other hand, I've written relatively few books on chemistry, which is my training. I've got a Ph.D. in chemistry, but I know too much chemistry to get excited over it, whereas astronomy is different.

BM: Excited. Learning really excites you, doesn't it?

IA: Oh, yes. I think it's the actual process of broadening yourself, of knowing there's now a little extra facet of the universe you know about and can think about and can understand. It seems to me that when it's time to die, and that will come to all of us, there'll be a certain pleasure in thinking that you had utilized your life well, that you had learned as much as you could, gathered in as much as possible of the universe, and enjoyed it. I mean, there's only this one universe and only this one lifetime to try to grasp it. And, while it is inconceivable that anyone can grasp more than a tiny portion of it, at least do that much. What a tragedy just to pass through and get nothing out of it.

BM: What happens to me when I learn something new, and it happens every day, is that I just feel a little more at home in this universe—a little more comfortable in the nest. I'm afraid that just about the time I'll begin to be really at home it'll be over.

IA: I used to worry about that. I said, I'm gradually managing to cram my mind more and more full of things. I've got this beautiful mind and it's going to die, and it'll all be gone. And then I say, not in my case. Every idea I've ever had I've written down, and it's all there on paper. And I won't be gone; it'll be there.

BM: Do you realize the possibility of that depressing the rest of us who can't write it down the way you can? Isn't it possible that one could say, "Well, since I can't write the way Isaac Asimov does and know what Isaac Asimov knows, I won't do it at all"?

IA: Oh, I wouldn't want people to do that. A little is better than nothing. In fact, you might say that I overdo it. Lately, I've been thinking that people must look upon me as some kind of a freak. There was a certain pleasure in writing one hundred books, you know. I felt I'd accomplished something. Then two hundred. But now it stands at 391 and it's liable to be four hundred by the end of the year—and I have every intention of continuing because I enjoy the process. And in the end, it seems to me, nobody'll care what I write, just the number. Maybe I will have defeated myself in that way.

BM: How do you explain yourself to yourself? What is it that caused a man to want to know so much that he would write four hundred books?
IA: Well, I suppose it's sheer hedonism. I just enjoy it so.

BM: Pleasure?
IA: Yes. I mean, what made Bing Crosby or Bob Hope play all that golf? They enjoyed it, and that's the way it is with me.

BM: Do you think it's possible that this contagion can be spread to ordinary folks out there—this passion for learning that you have? Can we have a revolution in learning?
IA: Yes. I think not only we can but I think we're going to have to. As computers take over more and more of the work that human beings shouldn't be doing in the first place because it doesn't utilize their brains—it stultifies and bores them to death—there's going to be nothing left for human beings to do but the more creative types of endeavors. And the only way we can indulge in the more creative types of endeavors is to have brains that aim at that from the start. You can't take a human being and put him to work at a job that underuses his brain and keep him working at it for decades and decades and then say, "Well, that job isn't there. Go do something more creative." You have beaten the creativity out of him. But if from the start children are educated to appreciate their own creativity, then probably we can, almost all of us, be creative. Just as in the old days, very few people could read and write. Literacy was a very novel sort of thing, and you thought that most people just didn't have it in them. But when you indulged in mass education, it turned out that most people could be taught to read and write.

In the same way, if instead of having mass education as we now have, must have, we have computer outlets in every home hooked up to enormous libraries where anyone can ask any question and be given answers, be given reference material on something you're interested in—from an early age, however silly it might seem to someone else—then you ask and you can find out and you can follow up and you can do it in your own home, at your own speed, in your own direction, in your own time, then everyone will enjoy learning. Nowadays, what people call learning is forced on you and everyone is forced to learn the same thing on the same day at the same speed in class. Everyone is different. For some, it goes too fast; for some, too slow; for some, in the wrong direction. Give them a chance in addition to school—I don't say we should abolish school, but in addition to school—to follow up their own bent from the start.

BM: Well, I love the vision, but what about the argument that machines, computers, dehumanize learning?

IA: Well, as a matter of fact, it's just the reverse. It seems to me that it's through this machine that, for the first time, we'll be able to have a one-to-one relationship between information source and information consumer, so to speak.

BM: What do you mean?

IA: Well, in the old days you used to have tutors for children. A person who could afford it would hire a pedagogue, a tutor, and he would teach the children. And if he knew his job, he could adapt his teaching to the tastes and abilities of his students. But how many people could afford to hire a pedagogue? Most children went uneducated. Then we reached the point where it was absolutely necessary to educate everybody. The only way we could do it was to have one teacher for a great many students, and, in order to organize the situation properly, we gave them a curriculum to teach from. So, how many teachers are good at this, too? Like in everything else, the number of teachers is far greater than the number of good teachers. So, we either have a one-to-one relationship for the very few or a one-to-many relationship for the many. Now, there's a possibility of a one-to-one relationship for the many. Everyone can have a teacher in the form of access to the gathered knowledge of the human species.

BM: Through the libraries that are connected to the computer on my desk in my home.

IA: That's right.

BM: But you know, Dr. Asimov, we have such a spotty—in fact, we have such a miserable—record in this country of providing, say, poor children even with good classrooms. I wonder if our society can ever harness itself to provide everyone, including poor children, with good computers?

IA: Perhaps not at the very start. But it's like asking yourself, "Is it possible to supply everybody in the nation with clean water?" Now, there are many nations where it is impossible to get clean water except under very unusual circumstances. That was one reason why people started drinking beer and wine—because alcohol killed the germs. If you didn't drink that, you died of cholera. But there are places where you can supply clean water for nearly everyone. The United States probably supplies clean water for a larger percentage of its population than almost any other nation can. It's not that we would expect everybody to have a perfect computer right off or to have equal access to outlets. But you try for it. And, with time, I think more and more will—just as, for goodness sake, when I was young very few people had automobiles, very few people had telephones in the home. Almost nobody had an air conditioner. Now these things are very common—indeed, almost universal. It might be the same way.

BM: So, in a sense, every student has his or her own private school?
IA: Yes. And it belongs to him or her. He can be the sole dictator of what he is going to learn, what he is going to study. Now, mind you, this is not all he is going to do. He'll still be going to school for some things that he has to know.

BM: Common knowledge, common data base.
IA: Right. And interaction with other students and with teachers—he can't get away from that. But he's got to look forward to the fun in life, which is following his own bent.

BM: This revolution you're talking about, personal learning, it's not just for the young, is it?
IA: No! That's a good point. No, it's not just for the young. That's another trouble with education as we now have it. It is for the young, and people think of education as something that they can finish. And what's more, when they finish, that's a rite of passage.

BM: What's wrong with that?
IA: What's wrong with it is you have everybody looking forward to no longer learning, and you make them ashamed, afterward, of going back to learning. There's no reason, if you enjoy learning, why you should stop at a given age. People don't stop things they enjoy doing just because they reach a certain age. They don't stop playing tennis just because they turn forty. They don't stop with sex just because they turn forty. They keep it up as long as they can, if they enjoy it. And learning will be the same thing.

The trouble with learning is most people don't enjoy it because of the circumstances. Make it possible for them to enjoy learning, and they'll keep it up. There's a famous story about Oliver Wendell Holmes, who lived to be well into his nineties. He was in a hospital one time and had not long to live—he was over ninety already—and President Roosevelt came to see him. And there was Oliver Wendell Holmes reading Greek grammar. Roosevelt asked, "Why are you reading Greek grammar, Mr. Holmes?" And Mr. Holmes said, "To improve my mind, Mr. President."

BM: Are we romanticizing this, or do you really think that Saul Bellow's character Herzog was correct when he said, "The people who come to evening classes are only ostensibly after culture. What they're really seeking is clarity, good sense and truth—even an atom of it. People," he said, "are dying. It is no metaphor for the lack of something real at the end of the day."?
IA: I'd like to think that was so. I'd like to think that people who were given the chance at learning facts, at broadening their knowledge of the universe, wouldn't seek so avidly after mysticism. I wonder how many people go for these mystical, nonsensical things simply because they must go for something and this is the only thing available.

BM: Mysticism. What bothers you about mysticism?
IA: The same thing bothers me about mysticism that would bother me about con men. I mean, it doesn't seem to me to be right to sell a person phony stock and take money for it. And this is what mystics are doing. They're selling people phony knowledge and taking money for it. It's wrong even if people feel good about it. And I can well imagine that a person who really believes in astrology is going to have a feeling of security because he knows that this is a bad day so he'll stay at home. A guy who's got phony stock may look at it, and it's nice and shiny with scrolls and old gold lettering and stuff, and as long as he doesn't have to do anything with it he feels real rich looking at it. But that's no excuse. He still has phony stock. And the person who buys mysticism still has phony knowledge, and it bothers me.

BM: What's real knowledge?
IA: Well, we can't be absolutely certain. Science doesn't purvey absolute truth. Science is a mechanism. It's a way of trying to improve your knowledge of nature. It's a system for testing your thoughts against the universe and seeing

whether they match. And this works not just for the ordinary aspects of science but for all of life. I should think people would want to know that what they know is truly what the universe is like—or at least as close as they can get to it.

BM: You wrote, a few years ago, that the decline in America's world power is, in part, brought about by our diminishing status as a world science leader. Do you still think that's so?
IA: Yes, I do. We're still probably well up there technologically, but what margins we do have are slimmer, narrower, and we're being overtaken.

BM: Why? Why have we neglected science?
IA: Well, partly because of over-success. I suppose the most damaging statement that the United States has ever been subjected to is the phrase, "Yankee know-how." You get the feeling, somehow, that Americans, just by the fact that they're Americans, are somehow smarter and more ingenious than other people, which really is not so. It causes you to rest on your laurels. It was first used in connection with the atomic bomb. The atomic bomb was invented and brought to fruition by a bunch of European refugees; you can go down the list of names. That's "Yankee know-how"? We think because we have what we consider a decent economic system, freedom, free enterprise, all that— which I'm all in favor of—that that alone will do it for us. I admit, that helps out in some ways—but not if we're lazy about it. It's not going to do it for us if we don't do anything, you see.

BM: And yet, there's always been a bias in this society against science.
IA: Well, it's against intellectuality. I mean, when nominee Bush can castigate Dukakis for going to Harvard, whereas he went to a proletarian school like Yale, you know there's something wrong. I mean, there you're actually trying to run a person down for belonging to what people see as an elite school.

BM: What did you mean when you said once that we have to stop living by the code of the past?
IA: Only because times change. In the old days, we didn't have to worry about the future, and now we must. We have to worry about the future all the time. Things are changing so fast.

BM: Is it possible that you suffer from an excessive trust in rationality?

IA: I can't answer that very easily. Perhaps I do, but I can't think of anything else to trust in. You say to yourself, "If you can't go by reason, what can you go by?" Now, one answer is faith. But faith in what? I notice there's no general agreement in the world of these matters of faith; they are not compelling. I have my faith. You have your faith. And there's no way in which I can translate my faith to you or vice versa. At least as far as reason's concerned, there's a system of transfer—a system of rational argument following the laws of logic, et cetera, that a great many people agree on. Therefore, in reason there are what we call compelling arguments. That is, if I locate certain kinds of evidence, even people who disagreed with me to begin with, once they study the evidence, find themselves compelled to agree by the evidence. But wherever we go beyond reason into faith, there's no such thing as compelling evidence. Even if you have a revelation, how can you transfer that revelation to others? By what system?

BM: So, it's in the mind you find your hope.

IA: Yes, and I have to say I can't wait until everyone in the world is rational, just until enough are rational to make a difference.

Isaac Asimov Interview

Irv Broughton / 1990

From Irv Broughton, *The Writer's Mind*, Volume II (Fayetteville: University of Arkansas Press, 1990). Copyright © 1990.

Isaac Asimov has been described as "the nearest thing to a human writing machine" and "a national resource and a natural wonder." A genius whose intellect is incalculable, he is clearly the most prolific writer in the world today. As of this writing, Asimov has written 395 books. Over the past eleven years, he has averaged over twenty books a year.

Born in Petrovichi, Russia, in 1920, Asimov emigrated to New York with his parents at the age of three. He was accepted by Columbia University at the age of fifteen and earned his B.S. degree from there in 1939. The war interrupted his doctoral studies, and he served as a chemist in the United States Navy until 1945. In 1948 he received his Ph.D. in Chemistry from Columbia. He taught biochemistry at Boston University School of Medicine but turned to full-time writing in 1958.

Asimov began writing science fiction at age eleven, and his first book-length work of science fiction, *Pebble in the Sky*, was published in 1950. He branched out into nonfiction with a scientific textbook published in 1952. Since that time, Asimov has written about an incredibly wide range of subjects from math and physics to Shakespeare and music. He has been a successful mystery writer, editor, journalist, biographer, and humorist. He recently wrote his 366th essay for a series in *Fantasy and Science Fiction*—not having missed an issue in over thirty years.

In addition to receiving a special Hugo Award (the Oscar for science-fiction writing) honoring his Foundation Trilogy as the Best All-Time Science Fiction Series, Asimov was given another Hugo for *Foundation's Edge*. In 1987, Asimov was the recipient of a special Nebula Award by the Science Fiction Writers of America, designating him a Grandmaster of Science Fiction. He has also received three other Hugos and two additional Nebulas.

As an interviewee, Asimov is friendly but business-like. He had agreed to forty-five minutes and, as if a clock went off in his head, his convivial side switched off and he concluded the interview. A prolific author obviously counts his time as precious.

Irv Broughton: Do you remember writing "Marooned on Vesta," your first published story?
Isaac Asimov: Yes, it was the third story I had written, but the first story I had sold.

IB: Did you have a certain confidence that story would be published?
IA: I can't recall that I actually thought that any of my early stories would be published. I only had hopes, but I recall my surprise and pleasure when it was accepted. I guess I must have really believed.

IB: Wasn't there a librarian who let you work in the library?
IA: I can't recall her very clearly. She was a very small woman, middle-aged, and not extraordinarily good-looking or anything—just an ordinary librarian. And I don't know whether she had ever heard of me. But I asked her please if I could stay there during lunch hour and type, and she let me. And she had no cause to regret it because certainly I didn't do anything but type during the lunch hour. I was not the kind of person who struck fear into people. I suppose I always seemed like a mild and gentle person so that they weren't afraid to let me stay somewhere. They weren't afraid I would get them in trouble.

IB: As a young writer did you envy any writers in particular?
IA: No, I can't recall that I did. I didn't have the kind of notion of myself that made me feel I wasn't getting the breaks I deserved. I didn't feel as though I wrote just as well as so-and-so. "Look at so-and-so getting rich and famous." I am extremely—I suppose you could say—"self-centered," but I like to think of me as a "self-aware person." However, my universe consists largely of me, so that I'm not particularly concerned about the success of others. It doesn't bother me. I'm concerned with what will happen to me.

IB: What characteristics of your parents do you have? I'm thinking perhaps in terms of the writing and the tremendous work ethic.
IA: My parents had that. They were poor people, and they were brought up in a nation that did not have any sense of caring for poor people. When they

came to the United States in the 1920s, it was a United States without welfare, without unemployment insurance, without any of the fixtures of the New Deal, which were later established. They knew and took for granted the fact that if they didn't work, they wouldn't eat. Therefore since they wanted to eat, they were intent on working hard. There was no danger that they would ever stoop to illegal methods of obtaining money because they were brought up in a strictly religious way. Without bringing me up in the rituals of the religion, they brought me up in the ethical content that they allowed. So I grew up expecting to work hard, and I have all my life.

IB: Did they introduce you early to literature?
IA: Not directly. They were unable to. They didn't speak the language. They knew nothing about the English-language literature. What they did do was get me a library card at the age of six and turn me loose in the library, take me there whenever they could. The first time they ever allowed me to take a bus on my own was so that I might go to the library. And all through, from the age of six to the time I got married at twenty-two, I was a library habitué. That was my introduction to literature.

IB: What was your library routine?
IA: The routine would be that I would go to the library, pick out two books or how much ever they would allow me, finish them, and at the first opportunity, return to the library and take out more and read them. I did this over and over. And, of course, my father ran a newsstand, and I eventually discovered science-fiction magazines at age nine.

IB: Describe the newsstand and your relationship to it.
IA: The newsstand contained all sorts of magazines. It was the heyday of the pulp fiction magazine where you had weeklies, biweeklies, and monthlies, with every kind of category of fiction: detective stories, love stories, western stories, air stories, jungle stories, hero stories—"The Shadow," "The Spider," "Operator Five," "Secret Agent x," all of which were out-of-bounds for me. My father thought they were not good enough. He insisted that I stick to the books that I got in the library. But then, in August of 1929, I noticed a magazine called *Science Wonder Stories*, and I sold my father on the notion that the stories dealt with science, so he thought I could read that. And then I read other magazines of the same sort, even when "science" was not in the title.

IB: Were there any other ways your parents tried hard to protect you in view of your obvious intelligence and potential?

IA: No, that was the one way. The other thing was that they approved of my doing well in school. And of course it's always nice to obtain approval of your parents. They didn't know the language, and, for that matter, neither my mother nor my father had ever received a secular education. They could read and write both Russian and Yiddish, but except for that my mother had no education at all, and my father only had a Hebrew education.

IB: You mentioned a specific month—August of 1929. Do you remember specific months and days in the way that the average person might not?

IA: I remember everything in the way that the average person might not. It's fading out as I grow older, but, when I was younger, I had a very remarkable memory, and as my wife said it's only now receded to the point where it's slightly better than average.

IB: How did you view that?

IA: I viewed that as though that were perhaps the greatest stroke of luck I ever had. It meant that I could learn quickly because people had to explain things to me only once. It meant that once I learned something I knew it forever. And it also meant I could pack a great deal into my three-pound brain, so that, in the end, I was able to write books of all kinds, on all subjects, and gain a certain amount of admiration therefore. So it's due to a reasonably high intelligence and a remarkable memory.

IB: You've pointed out, haven't you, that memory and intelligence are slightly different things.

IA: Oh, sure, it's possible to be extremely intelligent and yet have a very fallible memory. I've known lots of people like that. And it's also possible to have a photographic memory, a memory which is much better than mine, but which is not linked to any particular intelligence, so that you're merely a parrot, repeating whatever you've heard or read, without really understanding. I remember during the vogue for quiz games in the 1950s there was Teddy Nadler, who was a postal clerk, and who couldn't very well do any work more intricate than that of being a postal clerk. But he had this eidetic memory. He could remember everything he'd ever read, heard, and he could recall so that if you'd ask him questions and if they were quite factual: "What was the middle name of so-and-so?—he would tell you. But you couldn't ask him questions which were qualitative, such as "Explain the significance of American tariff policy after the Civil War." You know, he would draw a complete blank. Nevertheless, he was referred to as a genius. And it struck me at that time that is typical of the way in which people viewed intelligence. I mean, they didn't even know what intelligence was—they mistook it for a trick memory.

IB: How did we finally come to understand intelligence?
IA: I don't know that we—meaning people in general—ever do. Intelligence is an extremely subtle concept. It's a kind of understanding that flourishes if it's combined with a good memory, but exists anyway even in the absence of good memory. It's the ability to draw consequences from causes, to make correct inferences, to foresee what might be the result, to work out logical problems, to be reasonable, rational, to have the ability to understand the solution from perhaps insufficient information. You know when a person is intelligent, but you can be easily fooled if you are not yourself intelligent.

IB: One thinks of a Mozart, who was prolific in his work, and a Beethoven, who wrote little. How does one explain these things?
IA: Well, you're sometimes caught in the grip of whatever it is. I'm not prolific because I choose to be prolific, and I don't imagine that Mozart—with whom I do not for one minute try to compare myself—tried to be prolific either. It's just that in my case, stuff is always bubbling inside me and it bothers me until I get rid of it. And I imagine the same thing was true of Mozart. He had this music continually proceeding inside his brain, and it probably hurt him unless he got it on paper.

IB: Can you describe that hurt—the way you feel when you can't write because something intervenes?
IA: The closest I come is to say that the rest of the world recedes—that, as the thing tightens inside your mind more and more—you become less and less interested in anything else, more and more impatient with everything that's keeping you from the typewriter, less and less happy at not being at the typewriter—you're staring at your watch more and more. I mean, there have been times when I've hated to go to bed because I didn't want to waste my time. In fact, I suppose that what happens is you become very aware of wasting your

time. People say to me that I must be very disciplined in order to stay with the typewriter as much as I do. But that's not it at all. If I were disciplined properly, I could force myself to stay away from the typewriter, live a more normal life. The fact that I'm not disciplined—that I'm a slave to whatever it is that bubbles in me that keeps me at the typewriter—I suppose is the same thing that keeps some people doing nothing, instead of doing something, but it keeps me doing something instead of doing nothing.

IB: What's the most rigorous period of writing you've ever put in? Was there ever forty-eight hours straight?
IA: Oh, no. I've never done anything like that. I just write as I feel like, when I feel like, which is just about most of the time. But I got a lot done—not because I spent an unusually long time at the typewriter, but simply because I write very quickly and I don't revise much. So that, for instance, I have a weekly syndicated science column—each of which is eight hundred words long, and I always sent it in exactly to the line. And I turn it out every Saturday before breakfast, or if I eat a particularly early breakfast, immediately after. It takes me just about one hour from sitting down at the word processor to having the thing in the envelope ready to mail. And this is routine. I can type eight hundred words very quickly, and the editing takes very little time because it's usually fairly correct as I do it the first time. I don't have to brood about it all—it always comes out the same length to the correct line because I automatically pace myself so that if I seem to be coming to an end too soon, I put in another sentence. If I seem to be running too long, I cut out another sentence without even being aware of it.

IB: How fast do you type?
IA: I type ninety words per minute on the typewriter; I type one-hundred words per minute on the word processor. But, of course, I don't keep that up indefinitely—every once in a while I do have to think a few seconds.

IB: Ever had bad days where you have to think for quite a few "few seconds"?
IA: I'm pretty consistent. When I sit down at the typewriter, I write. Someone once asked me if I had a fixed routine before I start, like setting up exercises, sharpening pencils, or having a drink of orange juice. I said, "No, the only thing I do before I start writing is to make sure that I'm close enough to the typewriter to reach the keys."

IB: Baseball players get sore arms. Is there anything comparable for a writer—writer's back or typist's forefinger?

IA: I guess what we do is run the risks—aside from the fact of the sedentary life leading to overweight, flabbiness, which God knows I've suffered from all my life—of piles; hemorrhoids. I don't think I've got them but, you know, sitting down all the time is hard. And I imagine that you also have a chance of lower back pain which I occasionally suffer from. It may seem strange, but you get in cramped positions and you forget to change them. I notice that when I'm working on indexes and am bending over the cards—I do this for hours at a time—that when I try to straighten, I'm in agony. I guess the cure for that is to knock off every once in a while and stretch, walk around and loosen up, but you forget.

IB: How has the word processor affected you and the way you write?

IA: Well, it's cleaned up my manuscripts because I'm a pretty slap-dash typist, and when I type, although I say ninety wpm, it's not ninety wpm by professional standards, because professionals deduct for mistakes. And I don't. I do ninety wpm with lots of mistakes. And then, I'd go over my manuscript and I'd put it through the typewriter twice: first draft, next, go through and make minor changes, then type up final copy, and finally go over and correct the mis-strikes, and all the errors I make. So usually my final manuscripts are not as neat as a professional typist would do. And editors don't like it, but they figure, "Well, it's Isaac Asimov." However, now I do things on the word processor and edit as I go along so that I hand in clean copy. Also, when I do a book or a novel or a long piece, I generally do a first draft on the typewriter because I'm used to that. I work better that way. Then I put it into the word processor and clean it up. Even so, I manage to make a few errors that I don't spot when going over it on the screen, but not many.

IB: Are you a perfectionist?

IA: No, I'm not. You can either be a perfectionist or you can be a prolific writer—you can't be both. If you're going to start polishing and getting rid of every last little difficulty, you might do it, but it's going to take a lot of time. And I never have the time to take a lot of time. I'm much too anxious to get on to the next job.

IB: What was the hardest book to write?

IA: Oh, some I like less than others—some are harder than others. I once wrote a book called *The Human Brain*, which was very difficult to do because

I didn't really know enough. I had to educate myself as I went along. And my novels are generally hard to do because my plots are intricate, and I have to think up an awful lot of background, etc. Science fiction is more difficult than mystery fiction; fiction generally is more difficult than nonfiction. Nonfiction is easy if it's on a subject that I know about.

IB: The intricacy of plotting would seem to suggest that you would have to sit down and think it through before you sit down to write.
IA: When I first started, I thought I'd make an outline. But I couldn't stick to the outline because the story wrote itself. The outline was like chains, shackles, so I stopped. What I do is think up a general notion of what it is that I want to do. I think up a nice, snappy ending, figure out where I ought to start, and then make it up as I go along. And so far the intricacy always adds itself, and, when I'm all finished, everyone could swear I worked it out very carefully to begin with—but it's not so. Generally on page x I haven't the faintest idea of what will be ten pages later on.

IB: Do you have a plot that you're proudest of?
IA: The story I've written that I like best is called "The Last Question," but do I like it best because of its central idea or because of the details of its plot? I think it's because of its central idea. When it comes to plots, I'm much fonder of my mystery plots than of my science-fiction plots.

IB: Why is that?
IA: Because in the case of the mysteries, the plots are really the whole thing; whereas in science fiction the plots are only one-half—the other half is the futuristic society I've got in the background. That's what makes science fiction particularly hard. I have to juggle a society which is interesting in itself, and I have to describe the society in considerable detail without making the reader feel that I'm slowing up the plot unbearably. And I have to be able to tell the story without too badly obscuring the social background.

IB: Any incubation period helpful when dealing with a lot of research material?
IA: I never do have that—even in my nonfiction. I generally do what research is necessary and it's never very much. I still retain the ability to remember what I know, more or less forever, and to quickly glance over a scientific paper and get what I need and know it. I don't have to go back to it. So that

I'm not conscious ever of doing a lot of research. I do it, of course, but it seems to take place fleetingly.

IB: What was the easiest book for you to write?
IA: Well, if you don't consider just short books, a book that took quite a long time but gave the most pleasure was my autobiography because it dealt with something close to my heart. Next to that is something called *Asimov's Guide to Shakespeare* because I really enjoyed the plays and I like to talk about them. Earlier this year I published *Asimov's Annotated "Gilbert and Sullivan,"* which is a nice, big fat book. It sells for fifty dollars. And I wrote it in two months, in-between novels. And let me tell you, those were a happy two months.

IB: If you could have only one Shakespeare play, what would it be?
IA: Well, I guess it would have to be *Hamlet*, although *King Lear* runs a close second. And when I did the books I was surprised how much I enjoyed *Antony and Cleopatra*. I wouldn't have thought that would have been one of my favorites.

IB: Talk about the question of longevity. Would you want to live to be a hundred and fifty years old?
IA: Only if I could write. There'd be no purpose of living any longer than I can write. I can imagine an age at which my brain would have sufficiently deteriorated so that I couldn't write—even though I could still live and lead an aware life—I'm not talking about Alzheimer's or anything like that. But, if the time came when I couldn't spend all day writing, there'd be no point in staying alive. So to live a hundred and fifty years, yeah, I would like it provided I retained my mind in its full force.

IB: In its full force? What if you could only write a book a year, but it would be a brilliant book?
IA: I'd be extremely unhappy, extremely. As a matter of fact, when I had my heart attack in 1977, I didn't let it bother me at all—I was alive, I was feeling all right in the hospital, I wasn't in pain. Everything was okay—cracking jokes with the interns and stuff, until it suddenly occurred to me that the doctor was going to insist that I cut down on my output. He'd say, "Come on, Asimov. From now on, if you want to live, turn out only half." And I promptly broke down at that thought. But it was a breakdown for nothing because I never slowed down.

IB: You broke down?

IA: At the thought of having to work at half speed. It made life seem useless. And, as I say, I wasted my time breaking down because that was eleven years ago and, in those eleven years, I have not slowed down. As a matter of fact, at my heart attack I had published approximately one hundred ninety books— maybe a few fewer than that. Right now I've published three hundred ninety-five, which means that since my heart attack eleven years ago, I've put out about two hundred books, which is an average of nearly twenty a year.

IB: Think you could recite the names of all the books you've written?

IA: Oh, I think if I just sat down and thought about it, and just gave you this book, that book, and the other, I could list a good percentage of them. But I bet there'd be several dozen that I'd leave out. I'd probably leave out some of the anthologies—I've edited about one hundred anthologies, and they're not as close to my heart as my own books are. I don't experience them the same way I experience my own books. I wouldn't count them except that when I did my first couple of anthologies, I had no idea there'd be so many of them, and I automatically counted them. Because the number of my books has become a great point about me, people are always asking me how many books I've written. I don't count any book that may have my name in the title but on which I did no work at all. There are a number of books, which sometimes take three of my novels and slap them together. I don't consider that a book because I didn't do anything. But sometimes I put together a collection of stories, which I carefully select, to which I write headnotes, introductions. Every one of those stories may have appeared in earlier collections so they're just a retread, but, on the other hand, I did work on it so I count it. It would be very complicated to figure out which books are completely original, which are retreads, which are in anthologies, etc. And I figure the hell with it—I'll count them all up and leave it someday to some biographer to make sense of it.

IB: Ever puzzle over putting stories together?

IA: Yes, I did it yesterday and today. There's a fellow who wants to put out a collection out of my books and have me write a special story for it, which has never appeared elsewhere. I'll write an introduction and he would add illustrations. And then I have to choose the stories. I went through the entire list of my stories, and I tried to pick those stories which were not contained in more than one of my collections, did not appear in more than one anthology, and were not so poor—so early written, before I had achieved my maturity as a writer—that I was ashamed to have them included. I ended up with about twenty-seven stories for the book. That took considerable time, going through, making decisions—not the same kind of time as is spent in writing original material, but it takes time.

IB: When do you think your mind amazed you most with its abilities?
IA: Oh, I think my speaking amazes me more than my writing. I command high fees and I've received up to twenty thousand dollars—only once. My general pay is between seventy-five hundred dollars and ten thousand dollars.

IB: I read you didn't like to be referred to as a consultant.
IA: Because I don't consult. But on the other hand, I don't mind being referred to as an after-dinner speaker. In fact, I would describe myself as the best off-the-cuff after-dinner speaker in the whole damn world. I never prepare a talk. I get up and speak without notes, without rehearsal, without anything, and I do well. I simply, again, manage it through my remarkable memory. I remember everything that I want to say, and I think quickly on my feet. Last Saturday I was interviewed on "Open Mind," on the air. It was taped last June and what happened was I walked into the studio, sat down, and he asked me questions, and I answered. I did not know what questions he would ask. Yet, if you watch the interview, you'll see no hesitation on my part. Whatever question he asked, I answered. And that amazes me, frankly, that I can do that. I keep wondering how long I can keep on doing that. But it's much more remarkable than my writing because my writing I'm doing by myself and I can stop and think if I want to. But when I'm speaking on the stage or being interviewed—as for instance, you and me now—I don't have time to think, or at least I don't take time. I don't say, "Well, let me think about this for five or ten minutes, then I'll give you my answer." I generally start talking instantly and coherently. So how I do this I don't know, but it works and people pay me my large sums with smiles on their faces.

IB: At what aspect of your brain are you most amazed—is it memory, perception, reason?
IA: It's always been memory. I'm not continually good at the others. There are other people more perceptive; there are other people who are probably more intelligent, but there are very few people who have my faculties and

facilities where memory is concerned. And I'm so aware of how much easier it makes my life.

IB: You mentioned the quiz show a little while ago. Did you ever think of getting on one?

IA: I was asked during the fifties to be on a quiz show. I was strongly tempted. But then, I thought if I get on and win money, it won't get me much. People will say, "Of course." On the other hand, if I get on and make a fool out of myself—which can easily happen in front of a large American audience—I figure I would not like that. In other words, I had too little to gain and too much to lose so I refused to go on a quiz show. As a matter of fact, it turned out to be another one of those decisions I made purely for accidental or adventitious reasons which turned out to be right on the nose because when the scandal broke, I was completely in the clear. I'm perfectly convinced that, if I'd gone on, nothing on earth would have made me agree to fake answers or anything like that, but that doesn't mean that someone else would not believe that I had.

IB: Are there some things you wish you didn't remember?

IA: Oh, many things—wise-guy remarks I made, hurtful answers I couldn't resist making, unkindnesses to my children, to my first or second wife, people around. I mean, everybody does things sometimes in hot blood or out of mistake, because they think its funny when it isn't, and it's embarrassing to look back. And I must admit that I dislike my ability to remember every one of them.

IB: Did a lot of things stem from teasing?

IA: Well, some from teasing and some singly from the thrust or riposte of everyday life. Just to give examples that I remember of where I felt at the time that I was justified, but looking back I figured it wasn't fair. I was growing a mustache. I mean, every young man at one point or another tries to grow a mustache—or at least a great many. I did, and a young woman said to me when she became aware of the fact that my upper lip was bristling, "Are *you* trying to grow a mustache?" Somehow I interpreted it as a slur on my virility—you know, she seemed to doubt that I was capable of it, and so I said, "Why not, you've managed." And she had—that's the point. That was the cruelty of it. I'm sure she was very well aware, too, that she had a few scattered hairs on her upper lip. There was no call to say it except that at the moment I was too annoyed. Well, of course, she burst into tears and after a while I got to feeling very bad about it. It happened over forty years ago. As time went on, I learned not to do these things. But when I was younger, it was difficult.

Also, over forty years ago this happened. I've never had what you might call a trim body—I obviously lead a sedentary life, and it's only with great difficulty that I avoid overeating, so I've always had a kind of potbelly. And in the chem lab during the war, I had a rubber apron on, which kind of sloped down to my abdomen and then went over it and came down so I really looked humorous. I was busily pouring something from one vessel into another, and a young lady in the lab—a thin young lady—came along with a long glass tubing and presented it to me spear-fashion and said, "Isaac, I think I'll let out all that air in your stomach and make you look more like a man." And without looking up from what I was doing I said, "Use it to pump up your chest so that you look more like a woman," which was, again, a true remark, but not one which she appreciated. And she chased me out of the lab, and I didn't dare come back for the rest of the day. That sort of thing I can remember perfectly, and I feel ashamed of it.

IB: Give me another example.
IA: All right. This happened to me about two years ago. I was particularly ashamed of myself because I thought I'd cured myself of it. I was at a table with a bunch of other people. I was reciting limericks that I had written, and I recited one that I thought was pretty good. And the fellow who sat next to me said, "Oh, come on, you can do better than that." And I said, "The point is, old boy, you can't!" And the table burst into laughter. I felt bad immediately. I didn't have to wait and look back on it, but again, it's the sort of thing that I've tried to cure myself of, but it's been a difficult job. However, whereas in my youthful days until my middle twenties, perhaps, I was widely considered as a kind of insufferable, conceited boor; in recent decades I've generally been regarded as a nice guy. Of course, I'm a conceited, insufferable boor inside, but I just don't show it much anymore. (Laughs.)

IB: In a brief bio clip in *Is Anyone There?* you mention that you decided to get a Ph.D. in chemistry and you did; you decided to get married to a specific person and you did. Do you usually approach things that way or was that a little hyperbolic?
IA: No, it did happen precisely that way. It's not unusual. I generally decide to do things I know darn well I can do. I don't decide to become a champion

boxer; I don't decide to cross the Niagara Falls on a high wire; I don't decide to enter the Olympics. I know my limitations very well, and when I make a decision, it's something I've got a good chance to do, and it's something that I know my abilities allow me to attain.

IB: What does the future mean to you?
IA: Well, it means something either very bad or something very good, depending on what we do and what the headlines of the moment are. I feel good when there's any sign that we're going to be less belligerent toward others, as nations. I feel bad when the human species shows itself to be unusually stupid. I feel bad, for instance, when there's a race for the presidency, as there is this year, and instead of trying to argue out the future of the nation, you make a big deal over the Pledge of Allegiance of which I can't think of anything more trivial. Now both nominees never make a move without being surrounded by twenty-seven million American flags. I mean, I don't know which is sadder—that the nominees think this is a good thing to do or the fact that the American public would rather cheer twenty-seven million American flags than to consider: what are we going to do about these banks failing in the Southwest? What are we going to do about the balance of payments? What about the national debt? What about the possibility of increasingly hot summers? No one says a word about these things. You'd think they don't exist. What are we electing presidents for—to see who looks better sitting up in the American flags, for goodness sakes. I mean, what value is the Pledge of Allegiance? You take a guy who's ripping the government off in insider trading, in refusing to pay his income tax, in making all sorts of crooked deals. Do you think he's going to hesitate to pledge allegiance? He can put his hand on his heart and say, "I pledge allegiance to the United States . . ."—of course he can say it. It doesn't stop them from being crooks or villains.

IB: If you were forced to trade places with a great scientist, who would it be?
IA: The greatest scientist who ever lived was Isaac Newton, and he and I have the same first name. I might as well be him. Usually, for number two there is Albert Einstein.

IB: Are there any scientists who may be well known, but who repulse you?
IA: Oh, sure. Edward Teller. I mean, there's my idea of a scientific villain. I imagine that there are similar people all through history—not necessarily

that everyone would call them villains, but I do. There's a guy called Richard Owen who was an adversary of Darwin, whom I would consider a scientific villain. There are fortunately not many. By and large scientists, no matter how peculiar they might be in private life, usually as scientists are good men. Not always. There were German scientists in the post–World War I era who were violent Nazis. One was Johannes Stark, and the other—oh, my goodness, my memory! Why can't I remember it? Oh, Philipp Lenard. I always get panicky if I can't remember something. There's a guy called Cyril Burt and there are other scientists also—I'm only talking of scientists of international repute. For instance, Stark and Lenard were both Nobel Prize winners. Burt was knighted.

IB: Is there any scientific discovery you wish you'd made?
IA: Oh, well, who on earth wouldn't have wanted to have been able to write the *Principia Mathematica*, in which Newton worked out the laws of motion and gravitation. By all odds it's the greatest scientific book ever written—or ever will be written, I think. Who with any pretensions to being a scientist could not wish that he had written that book?

IB: Frank Herbert said he believed that eventually we'll leave this earth and live on another planet. Do you see that?
IA: We'll leave the earth and extend our range. That doesn't necessarily mean we'll abandon the earth. Europeans settled America and Australia—it doesn't mean Europe is less crowded.

IB: How important is the ego of the writer?
IA: Extremely important. There's no such thing as a modest writer. Just imagine that a writer thinks that what he writes other people will be willing to pay to read. It's as great an example of conceit as can be imagined, so that before a writer can even be a writer he has to have a healthy ego.

IB: Author John Baxter talked about how many science fiction movies in the past had as preoccupations the loss of individuality and the threat that knowledge creates. Yet, you're a person who creates knowledge.
IA: All through history people have been suspicious of knowledge—even in Adam and Eve's tale. Their great crime was to eat of the fruit of the tree of the knowledge of good and evil. In other words, they wanted to know something more than they should. And people have always felt that this urge to know

more than they ought to know is bad. But, naturally, I believe that is just the fear that is aroused on the part of people who are themselves ignorant, and who are afraid of people who know more than they do. I think that knowledge increases individualism, that the more we know the more we understand people as individuals, rather than just as members of a faceless mass. The tendency is always in the direction of recognizing the differences in people that you know more and more about.

IB: What were the origins of the story "Bicentennial Man"?
IA: A young lady wanted to do an anthology of stories, all of them suggested by the phrase "bicentennial man." She wanted to publish it in 1976 at the time of the Bicentennial. She didn't care what the stories would be as long as the words "bicentennial man" would fit somewhere in the story. And so, I wrote one called "Bicentennial Man." I figured if it was going to be a science-fiction story, it couldn't be this particular bicentennial, so what bicentennial could it be? I figured it would be someone's personal bicentennial—two hundredth birthday. I didn't think a human being could very well live to be two hundred, so how about a robot? So I wrote a story about a robot reaching his two hundredth birthday and everything else followed. Then it turned out that the anthology didn't work because—of all the stories she got—the only one that was useable was mine, and she herself had a great deal of personal problems, so the anthology never appeared. But the story appeared in another anthology that had nothing to do with the Bicentennial as a whole. But I guess the story was good because it won both the Hugo and the Nebula.

IB: You really predicted the idea of robotics, didn't you, in *I, Robot*?
IA: I was the first one to use the word "robotics." I was the first one to advance the three laws of robotics.

IB: How does that make you feel when you create knowledge?
IA: Well, generally I'm not aware I have until years have passed and then I'm more surprised than anything else.

IB: What's the most fundamental difference between art and science to you?
IA: Science is something that can be confirmed, that human beings can agree upon objectively. Art is something that is purely personal and subjective. One man's art is another man's trash.

IB: What were the watershed periods in your life?

IA: Coming to the United States when I was three years old, discovering science fiction, making up my mind to write science fiction, getting my Ph.D. in chemistry, getting fired from my job in 1958 so I was forced to be a full-time writer, then writing *The Intelligent Man's Guide to Science*, my first book that attracted the attention of the world outside science fiction, and finally, I suppose, getting my Grandmaster award in 1987, a kind of recognition of my life's work.

Isaac Asimov, Science Fiction Virtuoso, Dies

Myrna Oliver / 1992

From *The Los Angeles Times*, 7 April 1992. Copyright © 1992. Reprinted by permission of TMS Reprints for *The Los Angeles Times*.

Isaac Asimov, the biochemist and prolific author with an infinite imagination who penned nearly five hundred books of science fact and fiction, died Monday in New York. He was seventy-two.

Stanley Asimov, a vice president of *Newsday*, said his brother died early Monday morning at New York University Hospital of heart and kidney failure.

The author, who won a remarkable number of Hugo awards for science fiction, said earlier this year that a prostate operation had slowed him down, prompting him to suspend his monthly column in *Fantasy and Science Fiction* magazine. He had contributed four hundred columns and articles to the periodical over thirty three years.

Despite a heart attack in 1977 and triple bypass surgery in 1983, Asimov had continued producing ten or more books each year.

Once asked what he would do if a doctor gave him only six months to live, Asimov answered promptly: "Type faster!"

He told another interviewer that he worried about dying and having his brain decay, but cheered himself by saying, "I don't have to worry about that, because there isn't an idea I've ever had that I haven't put down on paper."

His final novel, *Forward the Foundation*, is scheduled for publication by Bantam later this year.

Fifteen of his novels, including the one not yet published, describe future civilizations spread throughout the stars, with solicitous robots serving humans.

Asimov set up the literary laws for fictional robots in 1950 in his second novel, *I, Robot*. The three laws were:

- Robots may not injure a human, or by inaction allow a human to be harmed.
- Robots must obey humans' orders unless they conflict with the first law.

- Robots must protect their own existence unless that conflicts with the first two laws.

Until the film world introduced the destructive *Terminator*, Asimov's laws had a definite softening effect on literary robots.

Aside from his science fiction, Asimov was probably best known for several factual science books, *The Realm of Numbers* (1959), *The Intelligent Man's Guide to Science* (1960), and *The Genetic Code* (1963).

In a 1988 interview with the *Times*, he left no doubt that writing always came first in his life.

"Everything else is done only occasionally and under protest," he said amiably. "Me and my typewriter, that's all there is in the world."

Typing more than ninety words per minute, he frequently worked twelve hour days and his output could easily reach four thousand words a day. Claiming it was easier to write new material than polish up old, he would abandon any piece if it required more than one rewrite.

Although Asimov translated and adapted a René Laloux animated film, *Light Years*, he generally eschewed science-fiction screenwriting.

"I'm really not a very visual person," he told the *Times*, "But also, I want full control of all my work. My books appear as I write them, and I've a feeling of ownership—even my editors don't argue with me.

"If I were to do a movie," he continued, "it might reach a hundred times more people than my books, but that movie would be a very diluted Asimov.

"Also, it might sound somewhat elitist, but I value the quality of my readers," he said. "If I only have 1 percent of all book readers, I have the best readers."

Asimov had no regrets about turning down Steven Spielberg's request that he write the screenplay for *Close Encounters of the Third Kind*.

"I didn't know who he [Spielberg] was at the time, or what a hit the film would be, but I certainly wasn't interested in a film that glorified flying saucers," he said. "I still would have refused, only with more regret."

Science-fiction films, he believed, wrongly sacrificed plot and storytelling for glamorous special effects.

"Frankly," he told the *Times*, "I'd rather sit at home and write my books."

One of his books, *Fantastic Voyage*, a 1966 novel about a medical team that was miniaturized and injected into the blood-stream of a dying man, was made into a movie starring Raquel Welch.

Most of his fiction stuck closely to scientific fact, but Asimov conceded that he slipped a bit with *Fantastic Voyage* because the miniaturized medics would have been too small to breathe a molecule of oxygen.

Asimov was born Jan. 2, 1920, in Petrovichi in the Soviet Union. When he was three, his family moved to New York, where his parents opened a candy store, and Asimov was soon reading the pulp science fiction novels they stocked.

"I imagine there must be such a thing as a born writer," he once wrote. "At least I can't remember when I wasn't on fire to write."

At fifteen, he graduated from Boys High School and enrolled at Columbia University, where he subsequently earned his bachelor's, master's and doctoral degrees in chemistry. Other than writing, his only occupation was as occasional instructor at Boston University medical school.

He began writing short science-fiction stories as a teenager and, after twelve rejections, made his first sale, "Marooned Off Vesta," to *Amazing Stories* in 1938.

During World War II he interrupted his education to work as a chemist at the Naval Air Experimental Station in Philadelphia from 1942 to 1945 and to serve in the Army from 1945 to 1946.

His first book of science fiction, published by Doubleday in 1950, was *Pebble in the Sky*, about a man transported by a nuclear accident from the twentieth Century to the Galactic Era 827.

Of *Pebble in the Sky*, Critic Margaret C. Scoggin wrote: "A nice satire on our own racial intolerances and our own militarists. . . . [The book is] well plotted with a minimum of jargon."

The science-fiction novels flowed after that, as did the Hugo Awards from the World Science Fiction Convention.

Asimov earned Hugos in virtually every category—for the best series of all time in 1966 for the trilogy *Foundation, Foundation and Empire* and *Second Foundation*; for distinguished contributions to the field in 1963; for science articles in the magazine *Fantasy and Science Fiction* in 1966; for best novel in 1973 for *The Gods Themselves* and in 1983 for *Foundation's Edge*; and for best short story, "Bicentennial Man," in 1977.

Further establishing him as outstanding in his field, the Science Fiction Writers of America selected his "Nightfall" as the best science-fiction story of all time in a poll taken in the late 1980s.

"No single author has ever written more books about more subjects than Isaac Asimov," *Time* magazine once noted of the man others have called "the writing machine."

Asimov married twice, first to Gertrude Blugerman, the mother of his son and daughter, David and Robyn Joan. After their divorce in 1973, he married psychiatrist Janet Opal Jeppson, who survives. In addition to his brother, Asimov is survived by a sister, Marcia Rapanes.

Index

Adam and Eve, 160
Afghanistan, 62
Alexandria, 131
Amazing Stories, 15, 165
American Association for the Advancement of Science, 82
American Humanist Association, 130
Ancient Greece, 110
Apollo 8, 6
Asimov, David, 166
Asimov, Gertrude Blugerman, 17, 166
Asimov, Janet Opal Jeppson, 166
Asimov, Judah, 17
Asimov, Isaac: on acrophobia, 13, 89–90, 102, 124–27; on the aesthetics of writing, 5–6, 22, 26–27, 29–33, 39–40, 43–44, 58, 59, 74, 76–83, 93–94, 99; awards, 105, 107, 130, 146; characters, 36, 38, 39, 42, 43, 44–45, 48, 51, 74, 104, 106–7, 122; on cloning, 117; on communism, 25–26, 59, 96; daily work habits, 16–17, 26, 79–80, 83–84, 95, 100–1, 151–54; on the destruction of natural resources, 138; early years, 15–16, 28, 46, 48, 57, 146–49, 157–58, 162, 165; education, 12, 15, 21, 45–46, 49, 57, 95–97, 139, 165; on energy conservation, 64, 67–69, 102, 116; as Grandmaster of Science Fiction, 146, 162; on his heart attack, 154–55; on human behavior, 23–24, 65, 98, 106–7, 135; influences, 29, 34, 52, 80, 81; on laws of physics, 23–25; on Marxism, 40; on mysteries, 36–37; office space, 14, 16; on overpopulation, 65–66, 67–69, 72, 118, 135–37; on his parents, 147–49; on Public Education, 92–93, 112–15, 140–43; on "pulp writers," 83; on religion, 52–53, 60, 85–86, 130–33; on robotics, 21–22, 24, 36, 52, 88–91, 98, 102, 115, 161, 163–64; science fiction, definition of, 58–59; on

science fiction and science, 5–9, 45, 134–35, 139–40, 150–56; on the sociological effects of technology, 59–69, 86–91, 108–19; on space travel and colonization, 7–9, 63–64, 69–75, 87–88, 106, 108–9, 118–19, 160; teaching career, 15, 16, 19, 34, 56–57; on telepathy, 102–3

Works: *ABC's of Space*, 18; *The Annotated "Gulliver's Travels,"* 105–6; "Asimov on Asimov," 39; *Asimov's Annotated "Don Juan,"* 96; *Asimov's Annotated "Gilbert and Sullivan,"* 154; *Asimov's Annotated "Paradise Lost,"* 96; *Asimov's Guide to Shakespeare*, 19, 154; *Asimov's Guide to the Old Testament*, 20; *Asimov's Mysteries*, 123; "The Bicentennial Man," 39, 161, 165; *The Caves of Steel*, 22, 27, 36, 51, 122, 124; *The Dark Ages*, 19; "Darwinian Poolroom," 50; *The Early Asimov*, 36; *An Easy Introduction to the Slide Rule*, 14, 83; *The Egyptians*, 19; "The Endochronic Properties of Resublimated Thyrathymalene," 11; "Enter the Neutrino," 45; *Fantastic Voyage*, 164–65; *Forward the Foundation*, 163; *Foundation Trilogy*, 21–23, 28–30, 41–43, 47, 48, 56, 77–79, 96, 102, 104, 106, 146, 165; *The Genetic Code*, 164; *Great Ideas of Science*, 18; *The Greeks*, 19; "Green Patches," 49–50; "The Greenville Chums at College," 15, 19; *The Gods Themselves*, 25–28, 165; *The Human Brain*, 152; *I, Robot*, 56, 161, 163; "In a Good Cause," 45; *In Joy Still Felt*, 21, 56; *In Memory Yet Green*, 56, 125; *In the Beginning*, 85; *The Intelligent Man's Guide to Science*, 162, 164; *Is Anyone There?*, 158; "The Last Question," 153; *Lecherous Limericks*, 96; "The Life and Times of Multivac," 82; "Life on a Space Settlement," 106; "Marooned

167